Called to Lead

catch the vision!

LINDA OSBORNE

© 2013 Linda Osborne. All rights reserved.

Unless otherwise noted, all Scripture quotations are from the NEW AMERICAN STANDARD BIBLE®, Copyright © 1960, 1962, 1963, 1968, 1971, 1972, 1973, 1975, 1977, 1995 by The Lockman Foundation. Used by permission.

Scripture quotations marked NIV are taken from the HOLY BIBLE, NEW INTERNATIONAL VERSION®, Copyright © 1973, 1978, 1984 by the International Bible Society. Used by permission of Zondervan Publishing House. All rights reserved.

Scripture quotations marked NLT are taken from the *Holy Bible,* New Living Translation, copyright © 1996. Used by permission of Tyndale House Publishers, Inc., Wheaton, Illinois 60189. All rights reserved.

Scripture quotations marked NKJV are taken from the New King James Version. Copyright © 1979, 1980, 1982 by Thomas Nelson, Inc. Used by permission. All rights reserved.

Scripture quotations marked KJV are taken from *The Holy Bible,* King James Version.

Scripture quotations marked CEV are taken from The New Testament of the Contemporary English Version: © The American Bible Society 1995. Published under license from Thomas Nelson Publishers.

Scripture quotations marked NCV are taken from *The Holy Bible, New Century Version,* copyright ©1987, 1988, 1991 by Word Publishing, Nashville, Tennessee 37214. Used by Permission.

Scripture quotations marked NEB are taken from the *New English Bible with the Apocrypha,* ©1961, 1970, the Delegates of the Oxford University Press and the Syndics of Cambridge University.

Scripture quotations marked Amplified are taken from THE AMPLIFIED BIBLE, Old Testament copyright ©1965, 1987 by the Zondervan Corporation. The Amplified New Testament copyright ©1958, 1987 by The Lockman Foundation. Used by permission.

Scripture quotations marked The Message are taken from *THE MESSAGE.* Copyright © by Eugene Patterson, 1993, 1994, 1995. Used by permission of NavPress Publishing Group.

The use of selected references from various versions of the Bible in this publication does not necessarily imply author or publisher endorsement of the versions in their entirety.

Published by Catch The Vision! Press
504 A Harbor View Drive, Klamath Falls, OR 97601

ISBN-10: 0615776582
ISBN-13: 978-0615776583

To my wonderful husband Bill, who made it possible, often through great difficulty, for me to follow God's call on my life. I miss you dearly and will love you always.

CONTENTS

	Preface	1
	Introduction	2
Chapter 1	Catch the Vision!	7
Chapter 2	Listen for the Call	17
Chapter 3	Follow the Leader	26
Chapter 4	Use Your Gifts/Part 1	39
Chapter 5	Use Your Gifts/Part 2	47
Chapter 6	Be Prepared	57
Chapter 7	Just Say Please	65
Chapter 8	Take the Lead	77
Chapter 9	Study, Write, Speak!	84
Chapter 10	Be Valiant	97
Chapter 11	Count the Cost	109
Appendix A	My Favorite Books!	122
Appendix B	Study Guide	126
	Bibliography	141

PREFACE

As you read my book, you will notice that I have often quoted from the book *Spiritual Leadership* by J. Oswald Sanders. Actually, several of the chapters included in this book were taken from messages I gave at a multi-church, weekly study based on the book. For me, *Spiritual Leadership* has been the most helpful and spiritual and even personal of all the books I have read on leadership. Almost every page of my copy is marked and dated with memories of things the Lord has taught me personally. As a result, I have come to consider J. Oswald Sanders as a spiritual mentor, particularly in regard to Christian ministry and leadership. For that I am ever thankful.

I also want to thank those living, breathing, active, and present mentors the Lord has so abundantly placed in my life. My mentors are my friends, and I have so many wonderful ones! I am truly a blessed woman. Each one has poured into my life some of what she has gleaned in her years of walking with and growing in the Lord. Some have gone before me in their walk and some have come behind, but each has helped to make me what I am in the Lord today. You know who you are; I am eternally grateful for each of you.

And finally, thank you to my beloved family who love me, support me, and keep me learning and growing as I move forward on this journey of life. I love each of you dearly!

INTRODUCTION:
My Story

I began to serve the Lord, really, as soon as I was saved. Only then it was simply sharing with others what He was doing in my life and encouraging them in theirs. That was always my favorite thing to do—and actually it still is.

When I was still pretty new in my faith, I started going to Bible Study Fellowship in Rialto, California. I knew nothing! I was like a fish out of water! I had only begun to walk with the Lord, but I realized that I wanted more! So, I began that study with another friend. That year they happened to be studying "Israel and the Minor Prophets." OH MY GOSH, was that a stretch! I had been out of school for several years at that point—it was September of 1976. I had never really studied the Bible before—other than a few home studies, this was it for me. And Bible Study Fellowship was like attending theology school! I remember that I barely understood the questions, let alone knew how to answer them. But I figured out something early on; I realized that if I only learned one thing each week, I would at least be moving forward—and that was enough for me!

The next year of Bible study I was asked to come into leadership. I began by teaching the children. Although I only stayed in that *position* for a short time, because of a conflict in my belief system and theirs (in the matter of the gifts of the Holy Spirit), I stayed in the *Bible study* for as long as I was able—even doing one study, "The Life and Letters of Paul," twice. I knew that, although we had a difference of opinion on the working of the Holy Spirit in our day and age, there was still much to be gleaned from the in-depth study of God's Word.

After six years of Bible Study Fellowship, I had graduated! And so, it was time to move on. That fall I began having a home Bible study with a group of ladies from a Christian women's group in which I was involved. But in the summer of 1983, at the end of that year of home Bible study, the Lord ministered to me that I wouldn't be part of that study in the fall. Now, I didn't tell anyone, we just said our good-byes for the summer, but I immediately began to pray. You see, in my short time of walking with the Lord, I had already begun to learn that if He was calling me *out* of one place there must be another place He was calling me *into*. And so I began to ask Him to show me where that was.

One Sunday morning there was an announcement in the church bulletin. My church, Harvest Christian Fellowship (at the time it was still Calvary Chapel Riverside), would be starting a women's Bible study in the fall. I remember reading that bulletin and *immediately* sensing that this was where the Lord was taking me. But there was just one little thing: I had been in Bible Study Fellowship for six years, and had been in leadership there; then I was part of another ministry, and I was in leadership there. I remember distinctly thinking that I would be going all the way back to square one—*again!* (I realize this was a little self-centered of me—but I'm just relating my thoughts at the time.)

Now, at that time I didn't know a single soul at Harvest. We had been going there for a couple of years at this point, and we did have a couple of friends that attended there—but they had just decided to start going to another Calvary Chapel closer to home. And in fact, when they moved I remember trying to get Bill to move to that church as well so we'd have some friends there. But he wouldn't have anything to do with that (and I'm sure glad now!).

So, there I was not knowing anyone and looking at the possibility of beginning a new ministry all over again. I went home that day and got on my knees beside my bed and I prayed to God and told Him, in a sort of whiny way, "I think this is what you have for me, and I like *that* part, but I feel like I'm going back to square one, starting all over again. It's like I'll be going all the way back to being a *very little fish* in a *very big pond*."

Well, the Lord spoke to me that day, right in the middle of my whining, and He said the simplest thing. He said, "You know what Linda, if I want you *teaching* that Bible study, then you'll be teaching it," period, end of sentence.

And then He laid on my heart Ephesians 2:10 (which I'm not sure I had even memorized yet, but there it was): "For we are His workmanship, created in Christ Jesus for good works, which God prepared beforehand, that we should walk in them." And with that verse, God gave me the scenario—*All I had to do was walk forward and I would come to every single thing He had for me—it didn't matter who I was or who I knew—He had the plan!* Now, how simple is that? So I got up off my knees that day knowing I'd be going to that Bible study.

There had been an announcement in the bulletin that there would be a meeting the next Saturday morning for anyone who was interested in joining the Bible study. I was excited now! I knew this was what the Lord had for me, so I told my husband everything I was thinking and asked him if he would be able to watch the kids so that I could go to the meeting on Saturday. Of course he said, "Sure," but when Saturday came along, something had come up, and he wasn't going to be able to do it after all.

Now, I must admit my first impression was to be mad and to say something like: "That's not fair! You told me you'd watch the kids! I'm *sure* I'm supposed to be at that meeting, etc., etc., etc!" And it's very possible that I got a little bit of that out, but the still small voice of the Lord intervened before I got very far, and I had the distinct impression that I was to be quiet and leave the whole thing alone. So believe it or not, I did leave it alone, and I trusted that the Lord had another plan.

Well, because I couldn't go to the meeting that day, when Monday came around I called the church and asked the receptionist if she knew how I could find out more about the Bible study. She said she didn't know, but she had the phone number of a woman who might be able to help me. Now, she just happened to give me the phone number of the woman who was helping my pastor's wife get the Bible study up and running. So I called her, and guess what? She just happened to be a former Bible Study Fellowship student! We ended up talking for a very long time on the phone that day, having a really great conversation, and in a very short time I received a call asking me to be a leader at the Bible study.

Now, remember I knew no one. Not one single person! And yet, I would be leading a group at this study. (Remember what God had said: "If I want you to teach, you'll be teaching.") Well, it seemed that the Lord wanted me to lead a group!

So in 1983, at the beginning of the Women's Bible Fellowship at Harvest Christian Fellowship, I was a group leader. The following year I was asked to be a Senior Leader—we had so many leaders that they needed a leader for the leaders! And during that year of Bible study, actually somewhere around the end of December, Cathe Laurie, our pastor's wife, asked a few of us to begin to pray about teaching the study the following year. She wanted to put together a teaching team. *Teaching*—isn't that interesting? That was the word God had spoken. I had *never* taken that literally—I thought He was just making a point! But evidently it was literal! So with great fear and trembling, I began teaching at the women's Bible study at Harvest in the fall of 1985.

One of the problems that we faced in the study was the lack of good Bible study material. The Lord began to place it on my heart that maybe we needed to write our own lessons. It sounded like a hard thing to do, and that was pretty much the reaction I got to the suggestion, but each time I let go of the thought the Lord would bring it back. I remember one night laying in bed thinking, "Yes, of course it would be too hard for us to write our own lessons—what am I thinking?" But immediately the thought came to me that teaching seemed like it would be too hard, but the Lord had enabled me to do that, and, really, wasn't it all the same? Well, that too was part of God's plan because in 1991, after much praying, fasting, and waiting on the Lord, a situation arose that sort of put us in a corner, and the only answer was to write our own lessons that year. That was the beginning of the wonderful privilege the Lord gave me to co-write the lessons for the Harvest women's Bible study.

In 1992 I was given another ministry opportunity, and I began to coordinate the Tuesday morning study, which was the study I started out with in 1983. This had been the first formal women's study at Harvest, and at that time it was quite large. We usually had between 700 and 800 women each week, with a large children's ministry as well (in the range of 400 to 500 children), and with a leadership of around 100 women. I had the privilege of going on staff at Harvest in the Women's Ministry department in 1997, which gave me the opportunity to be part of all the women's ministry there—but the Bible study was always my first love.

I have to admit that having such a rich ministry at Harvest led me to think that I had found my "life ministry"—and I even said that from time to time. But God has a way of surprising us, doesn't He? The time came when, by way of a very deep and difficult journey, He took me out of ministry there and brought me into a new place of service. Through this process I have learned a new thing (actually something I always knew—but now I just know it better!); I have learned that *I am simply His* and that He is free to use me wherever and whenever He will.

In 2009, I lost my beloved husband Bill. We had been married 35 years and I was so blessed to enjoy each and every one of those years. I have since moved to Oregon to be near my darling children and grandchildren, who have been a lifeline to me since our great loss.

Serving the Lord has been an ongoing adventure. I never know where He's going to call me, but I do know this: He has prepared my good works beforehand that I should walk in them. So I just keep walking!

> "But none of these things move me; nor do I count my life as dear to myself, so that I may finish my race with joy, and the ministry which I received from the Lord Jesus, to testify to the gospel of the grace of God." Acts 20:24

CHAPTER 1
Catch the Vision!

"We must work the works of Him who sent Me as long as it is day;
night is coming, when no one can work."
John 9:4

Do you remember when Jesus said to His parents, "I must be about My Father's business" (Luke 2:49 NKJV)? Well, that says, in a nutshell, what God has laid on my heart to share with you in this book. That is the vision I hope to impart—that we should be women who have made it our greatest priority to be about our Father's business.

Do you know what it means to *catch a vision*? It's when you see something in a profound way that you hadn't seen it before. It's sort of like getting a new angle or a new perspective on something that gives you a clearer and better sense of what it really is. You might even say it's like getting a glimpse of reality, and maybe, momentarily, seeing things as they *really are* from God's point of view.

In 1 Corinthians 13:12, the apostle Paul says, "For now we see in a mirror dimly, but then face to face." I think it's like that. We don't usually see spiritual things sharply and clearly—as they really are—but from time to time God gives us a glimpse of what reality looks like from His point of view. I had that experience several years ago. Just for a moment I saw something so real and yet it was just a glimpse. It was there one minute and gone the next, but for a moment I saw how important it is that we live our lives to the fullest capacity of usefulness to God.

I was at the house of a friend of mine, and we were talking about how much evil there is in this world and how much Satan and those he uses are accomplishing. As we were talking about the fact that Satan is indeed powerful, my friend said, "Think of that one woman, Madalyn Murray O'Hair, the woman who got prayer taken out of the schools. Look how much one woman was able to accomplish—and that for evil; think of how much more could be accomplished when empowered by God for good."

It was right then that I caught the vision. Just for a moment I saw so clearly that if Satan could accomplish so much with just one woman, how much more God could do with one woman (or one man) fully devoted to doing His will! And of course, it immediately became personal—just how much God could accomplish with *me* if I was completely given over to serving Him.

Can you catch a glimpse of that vision? Can you see how much good God could do with *you* if your life was fully devoted to accomplishing His will on this earth? Whether through teaching, praying, serving, leading, helping, administrating, giving, loving, or all of the above!

You know, I realized something that day after talking with my friend. I realized that I had become too careful. I had gotten to the point that I weighed and measured everything so carefully. Does this "good work" fit in with my idea of God's will for my life? Am I absolutely sure that this "new thing" really is God's will?

Now, it's good for us to be careful to determine the will of God, but I had become too careful. I remember a particular time that I had been asked to speak at another church. I said that I would pray about it and get back to them in a week. Well, as the week went on I kept praying and asking God to show me if He wanted me to speak there or not, but He simply wasn't telling me. The day came that I promised to let them know my answer, and I still didn't have my "yes." That morning, as I was having my quiet time, I was reading in Ecclesiastes 12, and I happened to look down at the bottom of the page and there was a footnote that said, in effect, that we are to use every opportunity to the fullest in serving God.

I knew immediately that was my answer! My answer was that I am to take advantage of every opportunity I'm given to use the gifts God has given me to serve Him. If God has given me the gift of teaching then He expects me to teach. And if I am asked to teach then it is His will, unless He shows me differently!

It reminds me of what Oswald Chambers says. He says, "The disciple who abides in Jesus is the will of God, and his apparently free choices are God's foreordained decrees."[1]

Samuel said something similar to Saul when God chose him to be king. Samuel told Saul that there were certain signs that would come upon him, giving evidence of God's choice of him as king, and he said, "when these signs come to you," in particular the sign of the Holy Spirit coming upon him mightily, you shall "do for yourself what the occasion requires; for God is with you" (1 Samuel 10: 7).

I wonder if you're like me, always careful to be sure that you don't step out ahead of God because you don't want to be presumptuous. Now, that is actually a good thing, and it's something that must be learned first before we can learn the second thing.

But the second thing is this: If we are abiding disciples (and that is the key here—we must be in an abiding relationship with God) and we're in the will of God, we can do for ourselves what the occasion requires when called upon to accomplish something for the kingdom of God, for God is with us!

Solomon said something of the same nature in Ecclesiastes 9:10. He said, "Whatever your hand finds to do, do it with all your might, for there is no work or device or knowledge or wisdom in Sheol (the place of the dead), where you are going" (Amplified).

This is almost funny! In other words he is saying, "Do whatever you can while you are here because you're going to die soon and then you won't be able to do anything!"

In Ephesians 5:15-16 Amplified, Paul says, "Live purposefully and worthily and accurately, not as the unwise and witless, but as wise (sensible, intelligent people), making the very most of the time, [buying up each opportunity], because the days are evil."

That day on the way home from my friend's house, I felt like God said to me, "Stop being so careful! If you only knew the things I could accomplish through you if you were totally abandoned to serving Me and accomplishing My will on earth."

Early in my walk with Jesus, once I had really become serious with Him, He spoke a word to me. It was another one of those moments when I had a glimpse into God's reality, just for a fleeting moment, like the one at my friend's house.

I was at the movies with my husband, and we were watching *Chariots of Fire*. I don't know if it was at a particularly inspiring moment of the movie—I found the whole movie inspiring—but at some point in time I heard the Lord, for the first time in my life, speak to me. He said, "I could do great things with you." Wow! That was an amazing word! Although I must admit I wasn't *sure* that it was Him, I had a deep sense that it was.

Maybe you've heard that same word. Maybe God has said to you, "I could do great things with you." You know the same potential is there for every one of us—the great good that God could accomplish with just one life totally given over to do His work and will.

Chronicles 16:9 says, "For the eyes of the Lord move to and fro throughout the earth that He may strongly support those whose heart is completely His." Don't you love those words? What a promise that is! I want to claim that promise for my life and my ministry—don't you? I want to be strongly supported! I need to be strongly supported! God has promised to strongly support the one whose heart is completely His.

We had a guest pastor with us one Sunday morning when I was still at Harvest. It was one of those mornings that the entire time he shared I was sitting on the edge of my seat because I felt as if he was sharing the very heart of a message that God was stirring within me.

The Scripture he used for his message was John 9:4, where Jesus says: "We must work the works of Him who sent Me as long as it is day; night is coming when no one can work."

Remember Jesus' words to His parents, "I must be about My Father's business"? And now to His disciples, "We must work the works of Him who sent Me as long as it is day, night is coming." That verse touched the thought that was in my own heart. The time is short! We must be about our Father's business! We must work the works of Him who sent us while there's still time!

Jesus knew He only had a certain amount of time to accomplish all that He had been sent to do. Did He accomplish everything? Absolutely! His final words were, "It is finished!" Each and every single thing Jesus had been sent to do had been accomplished.

John showed us this in his gospel, right before Jesus' final words. In John 19:28 it says, "After this, Jesus, knowing that all things had already been accomplished, to fulfill the Scripture, said, 'I am thirsty.'" All things had been accomplished. Jesus knew what each of them were, but in order to finish everything, one more thing had to be done and so Jesus said, "I thirst" and drank the sour wine. Then He was able to say, "It is finished! And He bowed His head and gave up His spirit" (John 19:30). Jesus had accomplished all that He was sent to do. He was done.

Now, we know there were a lot more things Jesus could have done. He didn't do everything there was to do. There were other people that needed healing, there were other demons to cast out, there were more opportunities to preach, but He had done everything that He was called to do, right down to drinking the sour wine.

Listen to what our guest pastor said about this. He said, "Life is too short to do everything we want to do, but it is long enough to do exactly what He wants us to do. If we think of all we want to do, we'll probably never get around to what He wants. There's not enough time to do both, but if we do what He wants, there's just enough time!"

In a biography written about Amy Carmichael, using her own words, her biographer tells about the time when she was called to the mission field and how those closest to her were having trouble understanding that God was calling her out. From the point of view that "we are not our own," Amy quoted from a song these words:

> "Not my own, oh, not my own!
> Jesus, I belong to Thee"

This is what she said about it, "though we sing it so often, we live it so little. We are very much our own, we don't live as strangers and pilgrims at all, and when the call comes to one to leave all and follow, it seems strange to us." And then she went on to say, and this is the point I want to get to, "We Christians have been trying to get as much as ever we could out of this life ..."

What an important statement! There was truth in those words when they were spoken, and they are still true today. We Christians are trying to get as much as ever we can out of this life. Amy goes on to say, "We have followed our Savior, it seems to me, very, very far off."[2]

In *Spiritual Leadership*, in a chapter called "The Leader and His Time," a little story is told about Michelangelo. "On one occasion when he was executing a work that he had been pressured into doing, someone warned him, 'It may cost you your life.' The great artist responded, 'What else is life for?'" Sanders goes on to say, "Our hours and days will keep on being used up, but they can be used purposefully and productively."[3]

The first half of that thought really strikes me. Our hours and days will keep being used up. Isn't that the truth? You can't stop it from happening, they simply pass us by.

One day you're 17, the next day you're 40; one day you have toddlers, the next thing you know they're grown up and having families of their own! The hours and days keep being used up, but they can be used purposefully and productively.

What are we using our hours and days for—ourselves and our pleasures—or for the kingdom of God?

One of the speakers at a "Preach the Word" conference, many years ago, made a simple point, but a good one. He said, "We all have the same amount of time in a day—24 hours—none of us has less and none of us has more; the difference is made by what we do with it."

And again from Sanders, a profound word: "We have each been entrusted with sufficient time to do the whole will of God ..."[4]

Isn't that great! You might say it this way, "We don't have enough time to do what we want and what He wants, but we do have exactly enough time to accomplish His will."

You see, He has prepared our good works beforehand that we should walk in them. Are you walking in them?

Most of you have probably seen the movie Schindler's List. It was about a man, Oscar Schindler, who had a job that thrived during the time of the holocaust. He used money that he earned during the war to literally redeem Jews—some 800 or more Jews who were headed to the gas chambers.

But even as he did this good work and saved so many Jews, still his vision was unclear, and he was fairly foggy about what he was doing. He was doing something which he knew was the good and right thing to do, but maybe we could say he was doing it somewhat halfheartedly.

On the day that the Jews were released whose names he had put on his list, suddenly he caught the vision! He realized that these people were being saved from death to life, and when he saw it—when he caught the vision—do you remember what he did? He broke down in tears. He suddenly realized the great importance of what he was doing, and with it came the realization of how much more he could have done. Suddenly he saw how many more people he could have saved, and he said something like: This car—100 Jews; this ring—10 Jews, and he started listing all the things he could have sold, realizing all the Jews he could have saved.

You know I often think that when we get to heaven that's how it will be. We'll suddenly realize how much more we could have done. Remember Paul's words: "For now we see in a mirror dimly, but then, face to face" (1 Corinthians 13:12)?

J. Oswald Sanders says, "It is well to consider the almost limitless possibilities of a single life for good or ill."[5] We can see the limitless possibilities for ill in the accomplishments of the Madalyn Murray O'Hairs of this world. But oh, to see the limitless possibilities for good in the lives of abiding disciples like you and me!

In fact, there are great possibilities for good to come out of your own life this very year in the ministry you are involved in right now!

Many times over the years I have had opportunities to do other things with my life. I'm sure you have too. Some were big opportunities that would have really reset the course of my life if I had gone that direction and not heeded God. And I will tell you that many, many times it was just after a temptation to go that different course that God opened up a new and even more wonderful opportunity to minister. I think they were sort of defining moments for me.

Some of the opportunities were just little things that didn't appear as if they would make much difference. And yet, it seemed that to God they did.

One of those little things happened while my daughter was dancing. I was asked to attend a meeting after a dance class where I was asked to take a position on the board of the ballet company. I was the only mom there who didn't work (although I worked very hard both at home and in ministry, but of course, that wouldn't have been apparent to them). Anyway, I went ahead and said "yes" to a position that I was assured would take very little time.

As soon as the meeting was over and I was leaving, all of a sudden I had the heaviest feeling in my heart. I knew it was God telling me something. I remember thinking that nothing was different that day except one thing—I had taken that position on the ballet board. And I also knew that the moment I got home I would get on my knees and find out what God was saying because I knew in my spirit that something was very wrong.

Well sure enough, when I got on my knees the Lord spoke. I was not to take that position. Of course that led to a little problem—I would have to tell my daughter's dance teacher—and I knew, instinctively, that I would have to tell her why! And I also knew, instinctively, that she wouldn't understand.

Well, the Lord ministered 1 John 3:1 to me that evening and this is what it says, "For this reason the world does not know us, because it did not know Him."

Yes it was true; she wouldn't understand. She doesn't know me because she doesn't know Him.

A day or so later, I was sharing with one of my friends what had happened, and she said the most profound thing to me. She said, "Linda, the world would love to have you, but God won't share you with the world."

That was a profound word to me! And I want to say it to you today: "The world would love to have you, but God won't share you with the world." Psalm 4:3 says it this way: "But know that the Lord has set apart the godly man for Himself." Be thankful that God doesn't want to share you, and remember the limitless possibilities of a single life (your life!) for good.

Every year as I entered into a new year of Bible study, I would pray and ask God to give me a Scripture for the year as my calling. One year the word was Psalm 18:32-36: "It is God who arms me with strength and makes my way perfect. He makes my feet like the feet of a deer; and enables me to stand on the heights. He trains my hands for battle; my arms can bend a bow of bronze. You give me your shield of victory, and your right hand sustains me; you stoop down to make me great. You broaden the path beneath me, so that my ankles do not turn" (NIV).

It is God who will strengthen you to do the things He's calling you to do. He will make your feet like hind's feet, and He will set you on your high places. He will stoop down and make you great. You see, He could do great things with you!

CHAPTER 2
Listen for the call

"Faithful is He who calls you, and He also will bring it to pass."
1 Thessalonians 5:24

If there is one thing we better be sure of when we step into a position of spiritual leadership, it is that we have been called. Not by a man or a woman or a church or a committee, but by God Himself. Because spiritual leadership is unique to all other leadership; the only way we can be certain of fulfilling the commitment is by knowing that we have received the call of God.

J. Oswald Sanders says it this way: "Places of spiritual ministry and leadership are sovereignly assigned by God." That is a powerful statement. And he goes on to say, "To be able to affirm, 'I am not here by selection of a man or the election of a group, but by the sovereign appointment of God,' gives great confidence to the Christian worker."[1] I have personally found that to be so.

As I have already shared with you, I was the leader of a large women's Bible study at Harvest Christian Fellowship for 12 years. As I called women into leadership, I had to be confident that they would fulfill their commitment to the study (which was for a period of around nine months of Bible study each year). I had to know that they would be there every week to fulfill their role, or maybe I should say to do their job. I had to know that they would be prepared each week when they came. I had to know that they would attend monthly leaders' meetings faithfully, and that they would be there early each Bible study morning for prayer, and so on and so forth.

Could I be sure they would do that for me? No way! But I did have the confidence that they would do it for God—if they knew He had called them. That was the key. And that was the secret to the success of the ministry—and it *was* successful.

You know, I am a person who will do anything if I feel that it's the Lord asking me to do it. Aren't you? If He lays it on my heart to fast, I fast. If He calls me to a ministry, I go there. And when I know for certain that He has called me—and that is the important part—then I will do whatever that ministry commitment entails. Aren't you like that too?

The key is to know that God is calling. Every year as the Bible study was winding down—around March—we would have a meeting and ask our leaders to begin to pray to see whether or not He was calling them back to the ministry for the next year of Bible study. We would ask them to pray and ask God to speak to them through Scripture, and, in fact, in order to come back into the ministry the next year, they were to get a scriptural confirmation from the Lord. I realize that this is a practice that might seem to be inhibitive or even a little too strict, but we found it to be a blessing on both sides. That verse was very important:

- ✣ First for me—because it enabled me to know whether or not God was calling the individual woman.
- ✣ Then for the leaders themselves—because it was by way of that Scripture and the other things God was ministering to them at that time that they knew that it was *God* calling them back to serve Him for another year in that particular ministry. And because they knew that *He* was calling, it followed that they had the confidence to believe that He would enable them, no matter what came up in their lives.

I can tell you that there was rarely a woman who didn't fulfill her commitment for the year of ministry—because her commitment was to

God. Although I'm sure they had respect for my position, and often they liked me and even wanted to please me, they knew that in the long run it was God to whom they were saying yes—not me. And that made all the difference.

When you commit to serve in a position in your church, I hope you will look at it from this same perspective: that when you commit yourself to ministry, you are ultimately and really committing yourself to God, and it is to Him that you are accountable.

That knowledge will do two things for you: First, it puts the highest priority on fulfilling the commitment you make. Second, it gives you great confidence as you step into the position you've been asked to do. Not because you think your pastor, pastor's wife, or ministry leader thinks you might be able to do the job, or that you appear to be someone who could do the job, but because *God has called you* to do the job. You understand that places of spiritual ministry and leadership are sovereignly assigned by God and that you are not in that position by the selection of men or the election of a group but by the sovereign appointment of God. That realization brings with it great confidence! God has called me so God will enable me!

Of all the verses in the Bible, the one that brought me the greatest confidence in my early years of ministry was 1 Thessalonians 5:24, which says, "Faithful is He who calls you, and He also will bring it to pass." I leaned heavily on the truth of that Scripture, and by virtue of the truth found there I was able to go forward and do what the Lord was calling me to do, even though I felt very inadequate in myself.

Now with all of that said—that it is God who does the calling and that it is God we serve—it is also true that when you step into ministry you are serving your pastor and his wife, because they are your leaders. They have sovereignly been given the position to lead and shepherd the body. They are the ones responsible to God for the ministry that takes place in the church. They will be the ones to whom God gives the vision for the ministry.

You will be following their lead, and you will be accountable to them as they are accountable to the Lord. Their God-given positions deserve and even demand your utmost respect. And in fact, your very position in ministry is actually an extension of the ministry of your pastor. You are, in effect, his arms and his legs, and he is the head.

If you can get that picture in your mind, it will help you to know your place and to be of the highest use to your pastor and his wife, as well as to anyone else God has placed in leadership over you.

I have always felt that when we understand that it is God who calls us to leadership we have a built-in respect for those in authority over us. We get the picture, so to speak. If there is sovereignty in the call to leadership, then we recognize that God has sovereignly called them to their position in authority over us. We respect Him by respecting those He has set over us. We serve God by serving them.

Now, let's look at the subject of motives in ministry. You know, you'd think this was something we wouldn't need to talk about but, actually, it is a very important subject.

In his book *Spiritual Leadership*, Sanders begins his first chapter with two Scriptures: 1 Timothy 3:1 NEB, "To aspire to leadership is an honorable ambition," and Jeremiah 45:5 KJV, "Are you seeking great things for yourself? Do not seek them." In other words, aspiring to leadership is an honorable ambition, but seeking great things for yourself is not!

Sanders speaks of a man by the name of Count Zinzendorf. Other than the fact that he was a count, he was a man that was very much like the rest of us, "strongly drawn to classical pursuits and tempted by rank and riches."[2]

So—he was drawn to and tempted by the same things we are: the world, success, money, and position. And yet, Sanders makes a defining statement about the count when he tells us that, "his attitude and ambition were summed up in one sentence, 'I have one passion; it is He, He alone.'"[3]

This man had a master passion—he had one ambition. It wasn't to be great, it wasn't to be powerful, it was simply to know Jesus.

I don't know if you realize it or not, but we are all, each and every one of us, influential people. You may not see yourself this way, but whether you realize it or not, the fact is that you are! You are influencing people every day of your life: your spouse, your children, your friends, your co-workers, and those under you in ministry. I think the statistic is that each one of us will influence something like 10,000 people in our lifetime! And in fact, another definition we could give for the word *leadership* would be, "the ability to influence others." Leading others really comes down to influencing others to follow you.

And you must realize that the kind of influence you are having on those around you has much to do with your master passion, your master ambition. Do you seek great things for yourself—success, money, position? Or are you simply seeking Him? It will make all the difference in how you lead and the kind of influence you are having on others.

Sanders gives a definition for the word ambition. He says that it speaks of "canvassing for promotion." And this is what he says, "True Spiritual leaders will never canvass for promotion."[4] Do you know why? They won't have to!

Remember Ephesians 2:10: "For we are His workmanship, created in Christ Jesus for good works, which God prepared beforehand, that we should walk in them." What an amazing verse that is! I've already shared how God showed me many years ago that all I had to do was *walk with Him* and I would get to every good work he had prepared for me. It's so simple! If we are walking with the Lord, abiding in Christ and in a right relationship with Him, our opportunities for effective service are already laid out on the path before us.

- ✛ Our job is to prepare our hearts.
- ✛ His job is to prepare our good works.
- ✛ We work on developing godly characters.
- ✛ God works on developing leaders.

Mark 10:43-44 says, "Whoever wishes to become great among you shall be your servant; and whoever wishes to be first among you shall be slave of all." Here we have that thought again of greatness, or of our desire to be great. It reminds us again of the Jeremiah Scripture: "Are you seeking great things for yourself?" and it makes us realize that there is a desire in us to be great. Now, that's not necessarily a bad thing. In fact, Psalm18:35 NIV tells us that God stoops down to make us great!

But Jesus helps us understand the truth about greatness. He taught us that, "True greatness, true leadership, is not achieved by reducing men to one's service but in giving oneself in selfless service to them."[5]

And of course, we know that Jesus Christ not only taught this principle but He modeled it for us. He is our greatest example of selfless servanthood. We'll be talking more about this in another chapter.

In his chapter "The Search for Leaders," Sanders makes this statement:

> "When God does discover a man who conforms to His spiritual requirement, who is willing to pay the full price of discipleship, He uses him to the limit, despite his patent shortcomings."[6]

Now we could have a whole chapter on those last three words, "despite his shortcomings," and I'm so glad he wrote it that way because if there is one thing we need to learn as we are called into service it is that we are used *despite* our shortcomings.

And if we are being used, it is not because we've reached some state of perfection but only because we have a heart that is turned toward God.

What is God's spiritual requirement? Well, I think it has to do with the heart. Remember that when God was about to anoint David to be the next king of Israel He told Samuel, "The Lord has sought out for Himself a man after His own heart" (1 Samuel 13:14), and that is the phrase that we affectionately apply to David—we call him "the man after God's own heart."

2 Chronicles 16:9 tells us that "the eyes of the Lord move to and fro throughout the earth that He may strongly support those *whose heart is completely His*" (emphasis added). I believe that God's spiritual requirement has to do with our heart being completely His.

- ✣ It isn't about talent.
- ✣ It isn't about education.
- ✣ It isn't about popularity.
- ✣ It isn't about looks.
- ✣ It isn't about how many Bible verses you've memorized.
- ✣ It isn't about any other tangible thing.
- ✣ It's about a heart given over to Him for His purposes here on earth.

And what does "one who is willing to pay the full price of discipleship" mean? Well, I looked up several verses which speak of discipleship to get an idea of what this would mean. And you know what I found? I found that Jesus has a very high standard for those who would be His disciples.

In Luke 14:26 Jesus says, "If anyone comes to Me, and does not hate his own father and mother and wife and children and brothers and sisters, yes, and even his own life, he cannot be My disciple." Pretty hard!

Matthew 10:37 says the same thing—but in a way that's a little easier for us to take: "He who loves father or mother more than Me is not worthy of Me; and he who loves son or daughter more than Me is not worthy of Me."

The idea here is that of preferring someone else (no matter how near or dear) and their ideas and feelings above the revealed will of Jesus Christ. And that can be a tough one, can't it?

Matthew 10:38 says, "And he who does not take his cross and follow after Me is not worthy of Me." And of course we know that the cross speaks of suffering/self-denial/death to self—another tough charge.

Luke 14:33 says, "So therefore, no one of you can be My disciple who does not give up all his own possessions." Yet another tough one.

Does this mean that you have to go home today and give away all your stuff or you can't be a disciple, therefore a leader? No! What it does mean is a willingness to have an open hand, to let Him take as well as give, and to follow Him and serve Him either way.

Matthew 16:24 says it best. Speaking of discipleship, Jesus says to His disciples, "If anyone wishes to come after Me, let him deny himself, and take up his cross, and follow Me." Follow Him where?

- ✞ To worldly success? Maybe.
- ✞ To spiritual success? Possibly.
- ✞ To places of difficulty? Likely.
- ✞ To places of self-surrender? Absolutely.

One of the principles that emerges in the book *Spiritual Leadership* is that there is a high cost to spiritual leadership. Sanders says it well when he says of the disciples that, "They must learn that for an influential spiritual ministry there would be a steep price to pay—and that it cannot be paid in a lump sum."[7]

If you are in a place of spiritual ministry, I daresay you know that statement is true and have already begun to pay that price. My friend Honey often said that each trial we go through is preparing us for the next. I've found that to be true, haven't you?

One of the things the Lord has taught me over the years—a simple thing really—is to *abide*. Learn to abide in Christ. Abiding speaks of acceptance and surrender to God's will, learning to live your life with Him on a one-day-at-a-time basis.

The apostle Paul says in Philippians 4:11-12: "I have learned to be content in whatever circumstances I am. I know how to get along with humble means, and I also know how to live in prosperity; in any and every circumstance I have learned the secret of being filled and going hungry, both of having abundance and suffering need." And in verse 13 he adds, "I can do all things through Him who strengthens me."

I wonder if you are *content* in the place God has you today. The answer to that has very much to do with what your ambitions are. If it's your ambition to be successful in the world and you aren't right now, then you're probably not very content. If it's your ambition to have some certain material possession (a couch, new carpet, a nicer dress, etc.) and you don't have it right now, you may not be content. Or maybe it's a better position at work. Or a certain person's respect. Or to be married. Or to have a child. Or to be a great leader.

Remember Count Zinzendorf—he had one ambition, he had one passion: it was Him and Him alone.

Listen to another profound word of the apostle Paul from Philippians 3:7-8: "But whatever things were gain to me, those things I have counted as loss for the sake of Christ. More than that, I count all things to be loss in view of the surpassing value of knowing Christ Jesus my Lord, for whom I have suffered the loss of all things, and count them but rubbish in order that I may gain Christ."

That, my friends, is powerful! What is your life's ambition? What is your master passion? Think about it right now. Identify the thing that keeps you going. If it is anything other than Jesus Christ, then you'll probably never have perfect contentment, and your usefulness to the Lord will be limited. If it is Jesus Christ—if rather than seeking great things for yourself, you are seeking first the kingdom of God and His righteousness—then you will be quite useful, and He will be able to pour His life through yours.

Of Count Zinzendorf it was said, "His followers drank deeply of the spirit of their leader and circled the world with the gospel."[8] I love the idea that they drank deeply of the spirit of their leader! Wouldn't it be wonderful if it could be said of you one day that your followers—your children, your neighbors, your friends, those you prayed with, those you lead and taught—drank deeply of *your* spirit, and because of your example they lived their lives fully for Christ?

CHAPTER 3
Follow the Leader

"Shepherd the flock of God which is among you,
serving as overseers, not by compulsion but willingly, not for dishonest
gain but eagerly; nor as being lords over those entrusted to you,
but being examples to the flock."
1 Peter 5:2-3 NKJV

In this chapter we're going to be doing a little Bible study on 1 Peter 5:1-4, so you may want to open your Bible there!

This is the final chapter of Peter's first letter, and you'll notice as you look at it that this chapter is very personal—really from Peter's heart to the heart of the reader. The actual message of his letter, as a whole, was concluded in Chapter 4. Chapter 5 is really just a series of admonitions, exhortations, and a final word of personal greeting.

Warren Wiersbe's outline of 1 Peter, in *The Bible Exposition Commentary Volume 2*, reveals that he sees this letter as a message of grace shown forth in *salvation*, *submission*, and *suffering*. And when we look at the final words of this letter, in this final chapter, we see each of those elements enter in. Submission is key; suffering is evident; and we're given a little glimpse of the hope of our salvation in verse 4, where Peter points to the Second Coming of Christ.

And if you think about it, isn't that even the theme of leadership?

- ✤ Submission is key.
- ✤ Suffering is evident.
- ✤ And every bit of our service to the Lord is based on the great hope we have of salvation. That's the hope that keeps us going.

Peter's message in this chapter is what we could call a word of exhortation. The word exhortation can speak of two different things. Sometimes exhortation can be a hard word—something that urges us to straighten up and fly right. Sometimes it can be an encouraging word, a word that brings hope and comfort. I've heard it said that exhortation is making the comfortable uncomfortable and the uncomfortable comfortable! I think both of these things are found in 1 Peter 5.

So, Peter begins his final thoughts by speaking a word of exhortation to the elders of the church or, in other words, the pastors among whom this letter would be read. But—for the sake of our study today and our own personal application, I'd like to open this up and look at Peter's words from a little wider view, from the perspective of leadership in general.

So take heart to the exhortation given in these verses in light of the position of leadership with which the Lord has entrusted you.

"Therefore, I exhort the elders among you, as your fellow elder and witness of the sufferings of Christ, and a partaker also of the glory that is to be revealed, shepherd the flock of God among you, exercising oversight not under compulsion, but voluntarily, according to the will of God; and not for sordid gain, but with eagerness; nor yet as lording it over those allotted to your charge, but proving to be examples to the flock. And when the Chief Shepherd appears, you will receive the unfading crown of glory" (1 Peter 5:1-4).

I love the fact that these few words of exhortation end by bringing our thoughts to our focal point—the Chief Shepherd. I love that title of our precious Lord. And right off the bat I want to point our minds in His direction as we consider what a leader should look like because He is our picture! He is our example! How did He lead? He was a shepherd. When Peter wants us to know what a leader should look like, he reminds us of the Chief Shepherd. In fact, Peter uses the shepherd picture all through this passage.

When you think of a shepherd, do you think of someone lofty? Someone highly important? Someone in a three-piece suit with a brief case and lots of important things to do? No! Of course not! You think of just the opposite. Someone lowly. Someone who, by the world's standards, is not so important. Someone humble, quiet, gentle. Someone who is more concerned with the little flock he leads than with the importance of his position.

We may not think of shepherds as too important today, nor did they in that day, but you know—it was to shepherds that the first announcement of the birth of Christ was given! And Jesus identified Himself as a Shepherd in John 10:11 where He said, "I am the good shepherd," and He looked at His own as His sheep.

Listen to how Isaiah 40:11 speaks of Him: "Like a shepherd He will tend His flock, in His arm He will gather the lambs, and carry them in His bosom; He will gently *lead* the nursing ewes" (emphasis added). I want to make a point here: our Shepherd leads, He doesn't drive.

In Mark 6:34, we are told that He felt compassion for the people, because they were like "sheep without a shepherd." And in a rare word of self-description, He said of Himself that he was "gentle and humble in heart" (Matthew 11:29).

Jesus, the Chief Shepherd:
- was born in a manger
- rode into Jerusalem on the back of a donkey
- put on a servant's apron and washed the feet of those He loved
- died a criminal's death on a cross, as He laid down His life for His sheep.

That is what our Shepherd looks like.

Now, let's consider Peter's exhortation. I want to begin by noticing Peter's humility in this passage. In verse 1 Peter says, "Therefore, I exhort the elders among you, as your fellow elder." I think that's an important statement. You see Peter could have said, "Therefore, I exhort the elders among you as an apostle of the church." And he would have had every right to begin that way. That would have given him a place of superiority and authority from which to speak to the elders.

But here as he was beginning his appeal to the leaders of the various churches this letter would go out to, instead of reminding them of the importance of his position, he *stooped down* from that place of great prominence and took his place alongside of them, calling himself a *fellow elder*, or we could say a *fellow leader*. The NLT translates it this way: "And now, a word to you who are elders in the churches. I, too, am an elder."

Another mark of humility in the first words of the chapter comes in Peter's word exhort. The very word he used for exhort in his statement, "I exhort the elders among you," is the word "parakaleo," which means to aid, help, comfort, encourage, call for, and beseech.

Peter was shepherding the flock even as he wrote this letter! He wanted to aid them with the very words he used: to help them, comfort them, and encourage them in their ministries. The word that Peter uses here is a close relative of another word that we know well, "parakletos" or "Paraclete," a word which speaks of the Holy Spirit, whom we know as Comforter (see John 14:16).

Why did the apostle Peter use such a gentle and humble word to make his appeal to these church leaders? I think it was because of what he was going to ask them to do. He was asking in the very spirit of what he was asking them to do because he was going to ask these leaders to be caregivers and comforters. And if you're called to spiritual leadership, that's what you are being asked to do as well.

Listen to the appeal in 1 Peter 5:2 (emphasis added):

> NKJV—"*Shepherd* the flock of God which is among you."
> NLT—"*Care for* the flock of God entrusted to you."

KJV—"*Feed* the flock of God which is among you."

Amplified—"*Tend* (nurture, guard, guide, and fold) the flock of God that is your responsibility."

CEV—"Just as shepherds watch over their sheep, you must *watch over* everyone God has placed in your care."

NCV—"I beg you to *shepherd* God's flock for whom you are responsible."

The word for shepherd here is "poimaino." It means to tend as a shepherd, and it implies the whole office of a shepherd—the guiding, the guarding, the folding of the flock, as well as leading it to nourishment.

J. Vernon McGee says that shepherding suggests: "Provision and protection, supervision and discipline, instruction and direction."[1]

Why did Peter choose this particular word, the word *shepherd*, in this word of exhortation? He could have said it other ways, but you know what I think? I think he was just passing on the call as it had come to him.

Do you remember the call? Jesus said, "Peter, do you love Me? Tend My lambs. Peter, do you love Me? Shepherd My sheep. Peter, do you love Me? Tend My sheep" (my paraphrase of John 21:15-17). Did Jesus have a herd of sheep we don't know about? Actually He did, and He still does—it's you and me!

Do you know what a pastor is? He is an under-shepherd. The very word pastor means shepherd. A pastor is Jesus' hands and Jesus' feet ministering to Jesus' sheep. That word for *flock* in verse 2 is actually translated "little flock." And do you see whose little flock it is? It's God's little flock!

And do you notice in verse 3 that he speaks of those entrusted to you or allotted to your care? That means the flock that is under your care is not yours, it's God's! They are His heritage! They are very important to Him! They mean everything to Him! They're the apple of His eye! They've only been *entrusted* to your care. You know—we need to be very careful how we handle the little flock that God has entrusted to our care.

Whatever place of leadership you have been given, whether within the church or without—this is the call. Tend My lambs, shepherd My sheep, tend My sheep. If you're already leading this way, praise God! But if you aren't, you need to be, and you need to start today.

Now, Peter seems to have three particular concerns in this passage. Let's look at verses 2-3 again. "Shepherd the flock of God among you, exercising oversight not under compulsion, but voluntarily, according to the will of God; and not for sordid gain, but with eagerness; nor yet as lording it over those allotted to your charge, but proving to be examples to the flock."

Peter wants his fellow-leaders to have the right heart in serving. He wants them to serve willingly, not grudgingly. Not because they have to but because they get to. It's a privilege!

I read an article, years ago, in an issue of Alistair Begg's newsletter, *truthlines*. It really said it best. This is what he says:

"When I was in high school in Scotland, the pool of soccer players assembled at lunch time on Fridays. It was then that we discovered who the eleven players would be to make up the team for the Saturday morning. I knew I was not one of the best, and yet I would sit and wait and hope for my name to be called and for the jersey to fly through the air in my direction. I would lay that soccer jersey with care in my bag and sleep with it by my pillow on the Friday evening. I did not care what position I played; I was so thrilled to be on the team. Today, as a pastor, Sunday by Sunday I feel the same way. I cannot believe I got picked. I think that's the way we are supposed to feel."[2]

Is that the way that you feel about the position of ministry God has given you? Do you see your position of leadership as a great privilege? Do you have to sort of pinch yourself in order to believe that you were the one who was chosen?

That's the way it's supposed to feel! It's a privilege to be called by God to serve His sheep. And if you don't feel that way, you should be concerned. (Now I'm not talking about being tired. We all get tired from time to time during the course of our ministry because it can be exhausting! But I always remember something Oswald Chambers said. He said, in essence, it's okay to be weary *in* ministry, but something's wrong if you're weary *of* ministry.)

In his book *My Utmost for His Highest*, Oswald Chambers has a devotion entitled "Are you Exhausted Spiritually?" The reference verse is Isaiah 40:28: "The everlasting God ... fainteth not, neither is weary" (KJV). And this is what he says: "Exhaustion means that the vital forces are worn right out. Spiritual exhaustion never comes through sin but only through service, and whether or not you are exhausted will depend upon where you get your supplies. Jesus said to Peter—"Feed My sheep," but He gave him nothing to feed them with. The process of being made broken bread and poured out wine means that *you* have to be the nourishment for other souls until they learn to feed on God. They must drain you to the dregs. Be careful that you get your supply, or before long you will be utterly exhausted ..."[3]

Peter's words in Chapter 5 are words of hope—and Warren Wiersbe says, "Hope is not a sedative; it's a shot of adrenaline, a blood transfusion."[4] Maybe today you need a blood transfusion in your place of ministry. Peter has the Holy Spirit equipment to give you one right here in this very passage!

Next, Peter goes on in verse 2 to give us the right *motive* in shepherding our little flocks. He says we're to do it not for sordid gain but with eagerness.

I was thinking of the day when a man is asked to be a pastor at the church—the great excitement he has! Or the day you were asked to be a leader at the Bible study. Or the day you were asked to take on a new position or job in the ministry. Weren't you just so excited?

Do you remember that day? The day God *chose* you? If you remember it, then you remember that the gain was the *position*. You had no thoughts of anything more. And that's how it should be.

Peter was concerned with those whose service in the church had become a *way* to gain—whether it be money, prestige, popularity, or power. And those things can never be the motive of our service for the Lord. In Philippians 3 Paul tells us that he counted all things loss, in order to gain Christ.

You know—sometimes there *is* gain in ministry:

- Sometimes you are elevated in position, and that's gain.
- If you're on staff, you might even get a raise in salary, and that's gain.
- Maybe the ministry is going so well and the Lord is blessing you and you're on top of the world, that's certainly gain.

But those things can never be your motive or your goal in ministry. If they are, I can tell you right now that you'll never go the distance because one day things may go differently. Maybe there will be *loss*—of position or of popularity or even of possessions. Is your heart the heart of a shepherd? If it is, then you will be able to continue on, in spite of the loss. If it isn't, then you'll be in big trouble. Check your motives: why are you serving? Is it for gain? Or, like Paul, is it in spite of the loss?

Peter also wanted them to serve as *examples*. Verse 3 (NLT) says, "Don't lord it over the people assigned to your care, but lead them by your good example." That word for "lord" actually means *lord against*. It means to control, subjugate, exercise dominion over, and overcome. It speaks of ruling forcefully. It's a word of harshness. This would never be the way the Chief Shepherd would have His under-shepherds care for His flock!

The Life Application Bible Commentary said something I thought was important. It said of that word *overseer* in verse 2 (serving as overseers, NKJV)—that we must "be careful not to read into the word 'overseer,' twentieth-century overtones of management, administration, and supervision."[5] You see, we are shepherding God's flock, not the *world's workers!*

In his book *Spiritual Leadership*, Sanders makes a great point about the word leader. He says:

> "In light of the tremendous stress laid upon the leadership role in both secular and religious worlds, it is surprising to discover that in the King James Version of the Bible, for example, the term 'leader' occurs only six times, three times in the singular and three in the plural. That is not to say that the theme is not prominent in the Bible, but it is usually referred to in different terms, the most prominent being 'servant.'"[6]

I love that! Who is our example in this servant leadership? Of course—it's Jesus!

Let's look at a few verses in Mark 10—because this passage is such a perfect illustration of Peter's exhortation.

✝ Verses 35-41—"James and John, the two sons of Zebedee, came up to Jesus, saying, 'Teacher, we want You to do for us whatever we ask of You.' And He said to them, 'What do you want Me to do for you?' They said to Him, 'Grant that we may sit, one on Your right and one on Your left, in Your glory.' But Jesus said to them, 'You do not know what you are asking. Are you able to drink the cup that I drink, or to be baptized with the baptism with which I am baptized?' They said to Him, 'We are able.' And Jesus said to them, 'The cup that I drink you shall drink; and you shall be baptized with the baptism with which I am baptized. But to sit on My right or on My left, this is not Mine to give; but it is for those for whom it has been prepared.' Hearing this, the ten began to feel indignant with James and John."

There they are, our beloved James and John, striving for position and seeking personal gain! (I wonder if Peter might have been remembering this little scene as he wrote 1 Peter 5.)

✣ Verses 42-45—"Calling them to Himself, Jesus said to them, 'You know that those who are recognized as rulers of the Gentiles lord it over them; and their great men exercise authority over them. But it is not this way among you, but whoever wishes to become great among you shall be your servant; and whoever wishes to be first among you shall be slave of all. For even the Son of Man did not come to be served, but to serve, and to give His life a ransom for many.'"

That's the picture! Whoever wishes to be great shall be a servant. Whoever wishes to be first shall be slave of all. Just like Jesus was. Is that the way we look at it? Probably not. It's certainly not the perspective of the world.

Peter makes an appeal to us—in fact, *he begs us*—to turn it around in our minds and get the proper perspective of leadership.

Jesus didn't come to be served but to serve. Are you looking to be served or to serve? Are you serving with mixed motives? Now is the time to check yourself, examine your motives, and make the necessary adjustments. The Chief Shepherd has entrusted someone into your care, be careful to serve them as He would. He is our example, and you are their example. Someone is watching you. Be sure they are seeing something that will help them when they become someone else's leader.

And the icing on the cake in our 1 Peter 5 passage is verse 4, where we're given the reward: "And when the Chief Shepherd appears, you will receive the unfading crown of glory." There's a crown waiting for you, servants of God!

The Amplified Bible says it this way: "And [then] when the Chief Shepherd is revealed, you will win the conqueror's crown of glory." I love that! A conqueror's crown! Peter is telling us that there's a crown in heaven waiting specifically for the shepherds of the church—for those who willingly and freely tend, lead, guide, encourage, and feed the sheep. That's the reward!

Do you remember how Peter said we weren't to serve for sordid gain? As I've already said, that doesn't mean there won't be *any* gain; in fact, there is plenty of gain in serving the Lord, but it's not often monetary.

I love reading biographies of people who were greatly used by God, and I remember on more than one occasion reading that one of these great men had been encouraged to go into the ministry by their families *before they were saved*, in other words, as a career.

Now by the grace of God these men *did* find the Lord and did eventually minister from the right heart and the right motives, but more often than not for very little monetary gain.

In fact if you go back and read some of the great biographies (I'm thinking of men like Hudson Taylor, George Mueller, and Rees Howells), which I highly encourage you to do, you'll find that the way was *always* hard, financially and otherwise.

So why did they do it? They did it because they passionately loved Jesus, because they passionately loved His sheep, and because of the hope that was set before them. They had their eye on the prize!

I've often said, kind of jokingly and yet truthfully, that you couldn't pay me enough to do what I do for the Lord for free. Do you know what I mean? Well that was their testimony. You couldn't have paid them enough to *do* all the things and to *go through* all the trials that they willingly and freely went through for their Lord. You see—they had seen His glory.

And that's the testimony of Peter in the passage we've been looking at. Look back at verse 1:

- ✣ Peter says he was a witness of the sufferings of Christ. He's speaking here of all that went along with the crucifixion.
- ✣ He says he was a partaker of the glory that is to be revealed. Peter not only would partake of that glory in the future with the rest of these leaders, but Peter had actually *seen* His glory on the mount of transfiguration, and that made all the difference!

I remember one Sunday at the church I was attending, our pastor had us stand up—*right in the middle of his message*—and give thanks and praise to the Lord. And we did! For an extended time everyone in that sanctuary was standing and lifting their hands and *loudly* praising and giving thanks to the Lord. It was phenomenal! I had never had that experience in church before! It was the most wonderful moment—and I felt the Lord's blessing over the whole congregation as we thanked Him, praised Him, applauded Him, and raised our hands to Him.

Now, that morning there was a boy sitting next to me that, for some reason, I had noticed from the moment he sat down. I can't explain it; he seemed to stand out to me. And in fact, I had it on my heart that I should give him a hug after the service. Now, this isn't something I regularly do, and I even wondered if he would be bothered or even offended by my action, but I still planned on doing it.

Well after our amazing time of worship, my pastor said something like, "Maybe the Lord has laid it on your heart to reach out to someone in the congregation today." I couldn't believe it! It was definitely a confirmation! And so after the service I stepped over to this boy and I said, "I believe the Lord wants me to give you a hug—may I?" He opened his arms to me and I gave him a big hug, and then I went to his mother and hugged her too. While I was hugging his mother, she said four significant words, she said, "You will never know."

No, I will never know—but the Lord knew. He knew on that day that for some reason (I'll never know that reason) it would make a difference in that boy's life if an ordinary person like me told him that the Lord wanted me to give him a hug.

Jesus loves His sheep. He knows every one of them by name! See to it that you serve His little flock in the right spirit and with the right motives because they are precious to Him.

And just a final word to you, in whatever capacity the Lord has called you to lead. Remember that word *shepherd*, because that's the picture. And when you have a question as to how to lead your little flock, remember to look to the Chief Shepherd. He is the example. His is the life we watch!

- ✞ Remember what He said about Himself. He said, "I am gentle and humble of heart."
- ✞ Remember that it's a privilege to be in the service of the Chief Shepherd.
- ✞ Remember the way the call came to Peter: "Peter, do you love Me? Tend My lambs, shepherd My sheep, tend My sheep."

CHAPTER 4
Use Your Gifts
Part 1

"For we are His workmanship, created in Christ Jesus for good works, which God prepared beforehand, that we should walk in them."
Ephesians 2:10

It is now time for us to give some thought to the subject of using our gifts. This chapter isn't going to be an in-depth study of the gifts, but rather my thoughts on the importance of using the gifts you have been given. We will do a more thorough study on the gifts in the next chapter.

I thought for many years (probably about 20) that I had found my niche. I had been given my ministry—it was the women's ministry at Harvest Christian Fellowship. Somewhere during the years I served there, I truly became convinced that it was my life ministry. But God sort of pulled that rug out from under me when suddenly, in 2000, things began to change. It was the beginning of one of my most difficult trials to date, but it ended somewhat surprisingly to me. It ended with my finding out a few things—things that I already knew in general, but things that became clearer than ever to me through that trial.

One of those things was that I became more aware than ever before that ministry happens wherever a servant of God goes. For a long time I had been in a very important and fruitful position in a very important and fruitful church. What would happen when I no longer had the safety of a title and a set position of ministry? This is what would happen—I'd remember the truth of the matter, which is that everything I do as a member of the body of Christ is ministry. It may no longer be as clearly defined as it had been for so many years (I believe I was spoiled by that!), but I have realized the value there is in simply serving Christ—whether that be by speaking at a retreat, writing a set of lessons, taking my mom to the doctor, or encouraging a friend on the phone.

My new motto has become, "I'm just His." That's it. I am simply His. He can use me as He likes—I am His to use however, wherever, and whenever He chooses. And I hope that He chooses to use me a lot!

Soon after I left my "set position with a title" ministry, I was in the beginning phases of learning to live without a huge and very time consuming agenda (although I must say, the Lord still seemed to keep me very busy!). We were at a new church, and I, naturally, began to go to the women's Bible study. I soon met some wonderful women who were very involved in the women's ministry and wondered if that was the direction the Lord was taking me. Although I made it known that I wasn't looking for a position, I sort of figured that would be the direction the Lord would take me, so I made myself available to help.

Now I have to interject here that I didn't really want to go that direction—in fact I had a sort of aversion to it (it must have been in my spirit) and so I wasn't hurrying that direction. But, because I assumed that would be where God would use me, I wanted to be open.

But the Lord had given me a verse as I left my ministry at Harvest—it was Joshua 3:4: "... for you have not passed this way before." In that verse, Joshua gives the people some advice. They are to follow the ark of the Lord, setting out from their place and going after it. But here's where the advice comes in: he says, "However, there shall be between you and it a distance of about 2,000 cubits by measure. Do not come near it, that you may know the way by which you shall go, for you have not passed this way before."

Use Your Gifts, Part 1

There it was—all of it. The *word*—you're going somewhere you've never been, and the *direction*—stay back far enough so that you can follow. In other words, don't get ahead of the ark, because you don't know where it's going! That was a very important word for me when I began my journey into this new unknown territory of ministry on my own. And I took heed to it! In fact, I was always aware that it was God's direction for me, and so I was very guarded about jumping out ahead in any way.

Well, one night at the Bible study there was a sheet of paper being passed around asking about areas we might be able to serve in the Bible study. I wasn't really sure what to do, so I signed up to help in an area that was sort of connected to what I had done before. I thought, well, if the Lord wants me in the women's ministry, maybe this will be a beginning.

In the meantime, at Christmas I had gotten a beautiful picture of a dear friend of mine and her family celebrating their 40th wedding anniversary. I couldn't believe I was hearing from her. We had gone to Bible Study Fellowship together 30 years before! And she had been a close friend of my sister-in-law, growing up. We had connected at BSF, and she had given me my first copy of *My Utmost for His Highest* (an act for which she will always be fondly remembered!). Very shortly after we met, however, she and her husband moved away. I had seen her a couple of times over the years at big women's ministry events and had given her my address. For some reason (the Lord!) as she was mailing out the Christmas card photos, she stuck one in the mail for me and Bill. When I saw the card and read it, I couldn't believe it when I realized that we were practically neighbors now that we had moved to Fallbrook. So I got on the phone and called her! We arranged a meeting very shortly thereafter.

I was immediately impressed with her wisdom. We both shared pieces of our ministry experience and realized that there were some striking similarities. She was a little farther along in her new place of ministry and so was able to give me some very good counsel. One of the things she said to me that day really stuck. She was talking about using our gifts, sharing with me what she perceived my gifts to be, and from the perspective of me being in a new church sort of tip-toeing towards the women's ministry, she said, "You know Linda, at your age you need to be using your highest gifts." That was the word. And it was a word from the Lord for me. It gave me instant direction.

I believe I've told Barbara how important it was for me that day when she spoke those words, but she probably still doesn't know the significance of it. It resounded in me as a word of direction. I knew that God was speaking.

At my age ... I need to concentrate on using the highest gifts that God has given me. For those of you who are on the other side of middle age, I would echo that word. *At your age*, you need to be using your highest gifts!

Now what do we do before we get to "my age"? In other words, how do we begin? Well, I think we begin by "blooming where we are planted." That is step one in serving the Lord. "Whatever your hand finds to do, do it with all your might" Ecclesiastes 9:10 Amplified.

It seems to me that there are two stages in our life of ministry. We start just by getting started! We do what needs to be done! Two things became important to me as soon as I became a Christian and began attending church: first—Bible study, second—serving God.

I had a Bible study in my little apartment before I had the least understanding of what it really meant to walk with the Lord. I was such an infant, but somehow it was inherent in me to gather together with others for Bible study, and even to serve—hence "in my apartment." I taught Sunday school when I didn't even go to church regularly (I won't mention the name of the church—they would probably not be too happy with that little piece of information!). I graduated from having my little apartment Bible study and began going to Bible Study Fellowship. I began to teach the children in my first year of Bible study. At that point nobody had even taught me that I was supposed to dive into the Word and fervently serve the Lord. It was simply what I was drawn to do.

What were my spiritual gifts? I didn't know! I hadn't learned much about any of that yet! So I served in the ways I understood, beginning with telling the kids Bible stories, helping at VBS, leading a home Bible study, then teaching a home Bible study. Little by little it began to come together. Leading and teaching were among the first two gifts I knew I had been given. Later I learned that God had given me the gift of writing. My awareness of my gifts only came out as I served Him here and there and everywhere.

As I've already mentioned (several times!), Ephesians 2:10 is one of my life verses. It says it so simply—"For we are His workmanship, created in Christ Jesus for good works, which God prepared beforehand, that we should walk in them." Although it's a good thing to discover what my gifts are and use them, really, if I'm abiding in Christ, it won't be too hard for me to fulfill my calling, because the path He is taking me down is the one on which my good works will be found and accomplished.

But none the less, after we sink our feet into Christ—being "firmly rooted and … established in your faith" (Colossians 2:7)—we begin to understand more clearly the gifts we have been given, and phase two of our ministry begins. Now is the time we begin to use those gifts, letting go of other "good works" that might keep us sort of spinning our wheels.

I remember very early in ministry that the Lord had to teach me this lesson. It was a time when I could see that there were many doors of opportunity opening, and I realized that I needed to start making choices—I couldn't go through all of them. It was 1984: the second year of my ministry at Harvest. I was running in circles! I had been given a bigger ministry responsibility that year, and I had two little children and a husband and a house and all kinds of friends. Now I always tried to be very available to my friends, and sometimes I gave them time that I really needed for other things. So I became stressed and wasn't the best wife and mom I could be. The truth is I didn't know how to say "no." 1984 was the year the Lord taught me how to say "no."

He spoke to me through my dear friend in ministry, Jan, who educated me to the fact that just because I was going to be home, didn't mean that I had to say I was available. I had the silly impression that unless I had an appointment or something, if someone asked me, "Are you doing anything Friday?" I had to say "No, I'm not," which made me available to them. This friend set me straight. Are you going to be doing your Bible study that day? Say that you're busy. Do you need to take time with the kids? Say that you already have something planned. I needed that! It sounds silly, but I needed to know that I didn't always have to be at everyone's disposal.

So that year I began to say, "No, I can't that day—maybe some other time," even if I knew that I'd be home and things would be quiet. I began to set aside days that I was "busy" being a wife and a mother, doing my Bible study, or even just reading a book!

About that same time, the Lord began ministering to me through Acts 6. The setting of the story is this: The disciples were doing everything! They were teaching and studying and also serving the tables for the widows' daily serving of food, plus probably a lot more than that. There started to be problems, because one person can't be responsible for everything and everyone. It turned out that the problem created a solution for more than just the widows.

This is what the passage says, "And the twelve summoned the congregation of the disciples and said, 'It is not desirable for us to neglect the word of God in order to serve tables. But select from among you, brethren, seven men of good reputation, full of the Spirit and of wisdom, whom we may put in charge of this task. But we will devote ourselves to prayer, and to the ministry of the word.'"

That passage spoke to me. I wasn't a teacher of the Word yet, and I had no idea that I would soon be called in that direction, but I knew that I needed to begin to make choices. With so many doors of ministry opening to me, which ones should I go through? I decided to do exactly what I had been called to do at the Bible study, and I began to say no to anything else that came along, unless I *truly* knew God was calling me to do it. I began to understand what it was to choose the *best* over the *good*. So, I devoted myself to prayer and the ministry of the Word, as it played out in the ministry I had been called to, and I let serving tables go. Now of course, if your ministry is serving tables, you serve tables. You do what you are called to do. I had been called to a leadership position in the Bible study, so that was what I needed to concentrate my energy and efforts on.

The interesting thing to me is that it was after this year of learning to say "no," and learning to make choices in ministry that the Lord called me to teach. I will never know for sure, but I think part of my preparation to be a teacher of the Word was what I learned that year. In order for me to live a life separated to the Word and to prayer, I had to learn to say no to other things.

So, I served as a teacher, a Bible study coordinator, and a lesson writer and the years went by—many of them—over 20 to be exact. And of course, I was getting older all the time! Now, *at my age*, I have found myself mostly writing, speaking, and encouraging others in positions of leadership. I have not ended up going back into women's ministry; I'm walking a different path—the one God prepared beforehand that I should walk in it.

One of the things the Lord has ministered to me about using my gifts is in the *Parable of the Talents*. For some reason, actually right before I went back to working on this book, I came across this story many times over. The main point of the story is to use the talents you have been given. The one man in the story was given five talents, he went out and invested them and made five more. The next man was given three. He went out and made three more. Both of them were praised for investing what they had been given and earning more. The third man was afraid of his master, so he buried his one talent, and in the end, returned it alone to the master. He hadn't used it and actually, by burying it, he had wasted what he had been given.

The point of the parable is that we are to be faithful with the different gifts and abilities we have been given. I use all that He has given me and I will be blessed. You use all that He has given you and you will be blessed. It encouraged me, again, to really step it up and determine to use my gifts to the best of my ability.

I was reading a great novel one summer, *The Copper Scroll*, by Joel C. Rosenberg. I don't often read novels, but because it was summer I wanted some easy and yet interesting reading, and so I picked it up. It's set in the end times, with the Antichrist about to enter the scene. The world is in crisis, and one character, who is more than busy serving the Lord, realizes there is no way he can do everything. Wondering which things of the many things that are coming his way he should do, he asks himself the question "how can I best invest my time until the end."

Now I don't usually underline in novels, but I found myself underlining and dating that sentence. And of course, I immediately prayed that prayer to the Lord: "How can *I* best invest *my* time until the end?" It was the word *"invest"* that really grabbed me.

I've spent the majority of my adult life doing ministry. Really, I can say that ministry has been my life! But that sentence made me think of it in a little different light. Not just, "What do you want me to do today, Lord?" But, "How do You want me to *invest* the time that I have left." I can't do everything there is to do. But I can do everything that is laid out on the path before me, choosing between the good and the best, and using my highest gifts.

I know that ever since I first read the *Parable of the Sower*, I've always wanted to be one on whom the seed was sown on good soil—the one who hears the Word and understands it and bears fruit—some a hundred-fold, some sixty-fold and some thirty-fold. I began praying, as soon as I first understood that parable, that I would be one who brought forth a hundred-fold fruit. I know you are praying the same way! And if you're asking for it, why wouldn't He do it?

What might God be calling you to do? How might it be that He wants you to invest your time? The possibilities are truly limitless! If you aren't already in the process of fulfilling your spiritual destiny, there's no time like now to get started!

CHAPTER 5
Use Your Gifts
Part 2

"And since we have gifts that differ according to the grace given to us, let each exercise them accordingly ..."
Romans 12:6

In this chapter, we will do what we didn't do in the last one—we will look at what the Bible has to say about the gifts of the Spirit. In other words, we'll do a mini Bible study on the gifts. But I want to say right up front that I am not an expert on this subject! You can go to your Bible bookstore and find many good books that will deal with it in a far greater and more defined and perhaps even more accurate way than I can (we must be open to the fact that this is a subject in which there are many different opinions and viewpoints—so let's try not to be too dogmatic!). My purpose here is simply to look at what Scripture tells us about the gifts and then to consider how we might use the gifts we have come to realize we have been given.

Let's begin by looking at the Scriptures that deal most directly with the gifts of the Spirit:

1 Corinthians 12:4-11—
"Now there are varieties of gifts, but the same Spirit. And there are varieties of ministries, and the same Lord. And there are varieties of effects, but the same God who works all things in all persons. But to

each one is given the manifestation of the Spirit for the common good. For to one is given the word of wisdom through the Spirit, and to another the word of knowledge according to the same Spirit; to another faith by the same Spirit, and to another gifts of healing by the one Spirit, and to another the effecting of miracles, and to another prophecy, and to another the distinguishing of spirits, to another various kinds of tongues, and to another the interpretation of tongues. But one and the same Spirit works all these things, distributing to each one individually just as He wills."

1 Corinthians 12:28-30 adds—
"And God has appointed in the church, first apostles, second prophets, third teachers, then miracles, then gifts of healings, helps, administrations, various kinds of tongues. All are not apostles, are they? All are not prophets, are they? All are not teachers, are they? All are not workers of miracles, are they? All do not have gifts of healings, do they? All do not speak with tongues, do they? All do not interpret, do they?"

Let's stop for a moment and look at four important things we need to know about the gifts:

First—Gifts are given by the Holy Spirit at His discretion. 1 Corinthians 12:11 says, "But one and the same Spirit works all these things, distributing to each one individually *just as He wills*" (emphasis added).

Second— Each of us has a unique set of gifts, according to the discretion of the Holy Spirit. 1 Corinthians 12:29 says, "All are not apostles, are they? All are not prophets, are they? All are not workers of miracles, are they?" The question is obviously rhetorical. The answer is no.

Third— Every Christian has at least one, if not several spiritual gifts—as we read in that same verse that they are distributed to each one individually. And 1 Peter 4:10 says, "As *each one* has received a special gift, employ it in serving one another, as good stewards of the manifold grace of God" (emphasis added).

Fourth—Spiritual gifts are given specifically to benefit the body of Christ. 1 Corinthians 12:7 says, "But to one is given the manifestation of the Spirit *for the common good*" (emphasis added).

Romans 12:6-8 continues with more instruction on the gifts—
"And since we have gifts that differ according to the grace given to us, let each exercise them accordingly: if prophecy, according to the proportion of his faith; if service, in his serving; or he who teaches, in his teaching; or he who exhorts, in his exhortation; he who gives, with liberality; he who leads, with diligence; he who shows mercy, with cheerfulness."

Ephesians 4:11-12 tells us—
"And He gave some as apostles, and some as prophets, and some as evangelists, and some as pastors and teachers, for the equipping of the saints for the work of service, to the building up of the body of Christ ..."

When I was studying Ephesians 4 some years ago, I saw something I had never seen before. I realized that this passage wasn't simply speaking of God giving certain gifts to the church, but these verses tell us that He gave *gifted men* to the church: apostles, prophets, evangelists, pastors, and teachers; along with the gifts of helps, the word of knowledge, the word of wisdom, exhortation, giving, faith, leading, healing, mercy, miracles, discernment, tongues, and interpretation. I want to take a few of these gifts and share a little bit about them.

Gifts such as apostleship, healing, and miracles are gifts that are not in operation in exactly the same way they were originally. The original gift of apostleship was more an office than a gift. In its first official use, this spoke only of the original 12 apostles. Secondarily and unofficially, others were included in that title: Paul, Barnabas, James—the Lord's brother, Silvanus, and Timothy. At this point in time, it is not an office but a function. Today it seems to be applied most often to the missionary or to the one who establishes and strengthens churches.

Although God does indeed still heal and work miracles (praise Him for that!), both of these gifts were originally known as "signifying" gifts for the authentification of the Deity of Christ during His earthly ministry and after that to confirm the authority of the ministry of the apostles. Today we call them manifestation gifts—as they are supernatural manifestations of the Holy Spirit. Praise God that He does still heal, and anyone who is an abiding follower of Christ has probably seen many miracles by now—I know I have!

The gift of prophecy is a gift that has changed over the course of time. In pre-Bible times—before we had the written Word of God—the prophet proclaimed that which had not yet been revealed. Today, the prophet is one who proclaims the Word of God—especially emphasizing the need for holiness. We might say that in the past prophecy was a new truth revealed and in the present it is a revealed truth proclaimed (perhaps at a particularly significant time for a particularly significant work or message).

Prophecy, along with pastoring, teaching, evangelism, and exhortation, is considered a speaking gift. The word we might use to define prophecy today is preaching. In their book *Discovering your God-Given Gifts*, Don and Katie Fortune have labeled the person possessing this gift, as it applies to the motivational gift given in Romans 12, as the perceiver, defining him as "one who clearly perceives the will of God."[1]

The difference between the gifts of teaching and prophesying is that the teacher begins with the desire to expound the Word of God, whereas the prophet begins with a desire to expose sin and produce holiness.

The gift of discernment is the ability to discern between the spirit of truth and the spirit of error. It is the ability to discern the wrong motive as well as the wrong message. Remember in Acts, when the slave-girl was following Paul around for days saying, "These men are bond-servants of the Most High God, who are proclaiming to you the way of salvation" (Acts 16:17)? Paul rebuked her and commanded an evil spirit to come out of her, in the name of Jesus. He had the discernment to see that, although what she was saying was right, she was filled with an evil spirit.

The spirit of discernment can give one the ability to sense the presence of evil. My daughter has had that experience many times. I remember once, she went with a friend to San Francisco, and she asked me to pray for her, because she always struggled when she was staying in a hotel. I remember as I prayed for her about this problem she seemed to have, the Lord revealed to me that it was because of the gift of discernment.

Another time she and I were in a city I won't mention by name, because so many of you (like me) love it there. But it is very "new-agey." We were walking down the main street of shops, and she mentioned that she wasn't feeling good about things. When we went into a particular shop, she couldn't even stay there—and I even felt that one!

There are those who believe that you either have this gift or you don't, and there are those who believe that it isn't a permanent gift, but one that comes to a person if and when the Holy Spirit chooses. I have a hard time not believing both! If it is only momentarily, at the bidding of the Holy Spirit, then for some reason He uses this gift often with my daughter. And conversely, I don't often have the discernment of spirits, but I definitely do from time to time.

The NLT says this of the word of wisdom: "To one person the Spirit gives the ability to give wise advice" (1 Corinthians 12:8). That sort of simplifies the gift. But it is anything but simple if you are the recipient of a word of wisdom—because it is of the supernatural order! It is actually the Holy Spirit giving the speaker a revelation of wisdom for the person he or she is sharing with.

Of the word of knowledge, the NLT says, "to another He gives the gift of special knowledge" (1 Corinthians 12:8). This, again, is a supernatural revelation of the Holy Spirit concerning information that the speaker could not have known. The word of knowledge is most commonly given for the purpose of prayer: the one who "sees" something that he or she could not have otherwise known can pray in this light for the one about whom the word of knowledge was given.

The gift of faith is the ability to believe God for the impossible. Again, it is a supernatural enabling. The Bible teaches us that we all have a measure of faith, and that as we exercise our faith, it grows. Hopefully you have already seen this to be true in your own life. But the gift of faith is given at particular moments in time so that the recipient can have faith for something impossible. Here are a few examples of people who operated in this gift:

- George Mueller, who took care of over 10,000 orphans in England in the 1800s.
- Hudson Taylor, who founded the China Inland Mission amidst very strong and constant opposition.
- Amy Carmichael, who saved little children in India from temple prostitution.

This gift enables men and women to do great things for God. People who exercise this gift are usually people who have vision. One of the signs that this gift is operating in your life is that you are able to believe God for that which appears to be impossible. Again, because this is what is known as a "manifestation gift," it is probably not so much a lifetime gift as it is the temporary gifting of the Holy Spirit for the impossible situation.

The gift of exhortation is often called the gift of encouragement. It is a motivational gift used by God to stimulate the faith and personal growth of others. Although it is often used on a one-to-one basis, this gift is also used in teaching. Sometimes the person teaching is actually operating in the gift of exhortation.

The gift of teaching is the gift of instruction. It is the ability to explain and apply Christian doctrine. I believe that writing—the gift which I most enjoy—is an extension of the gift of teaching. And I'm not the only writer in my family—I'm looking for my son to be publishing a book one of these days! And both my daughter-in-law and son-in-law are teachers by profession.

The gift of administrations and/or leadership is, in its most simple state, the gift of management. The one with this gift guides or governs others and has the ability to organize.

What we often call the gift of helps is actually the gift of service. It is the Spirit-given ability to serve the church in a supporting role. It is one of the most widely held and one of the most diversified of the gifts. Although everyone who uses their God-given gifts is a servant, this gift may be the most obvious of the "servant" gifts.

Most often the person with the gift of helps is a behind-the-scenes worker. The beauty of this gift is that it frees up others in the church to use their gifts.

I think this is my mom's gift. In particular, I would say she has the gift of hospitality. That's why someone at her church asked her to greet on Sunday mornings. They could see this gift in her!

The gift of giving is pretty self-explanatory. It is the Spirit-given ability to share cheerfully and generously to further the work of God. Many times a person with this gift is a wealthy person who is able to give liberally to God's work. If you have ever done one of the tests on spiritual gifts that many churches and books provide, you will usually see this gift applied that way—to the wealthy individual who gives generously to others.

But don't let that fool you! There are many, many people who have limited incomes and yet operate fluently in this gift. My husband is my case in point. He had the gift of giving. I don't! Now don't get me wrong—I love to give to others when I see a need that I can help with. But there was something in my husband that was unusual, you see, he was compelled to give. He couldn't not give! In fact, one day many years ago we had a conversation that went something like this:

"You know Bill, you really do need to be more careful with how you give out money. We have some new bills and our finances are a little stretched, so you really need to take that into consideration when you feel the urge to give."

He listened to all of that (and much more—we were on the way to church, so I had a lot of time to talk!). When I finished he said something like this:

"I hear what you're saying, and I understand where you're coming from. But I really think I need to just let the Lord show me when and where to give." End of discussion.

The one who has the gift of giving, whether they give $20.00 and a ride to the bus station or thousands of dollars to a missionary organization, are none-the-less compelled by the Spirit of God to give. And when they give, it is generously and without ulterior motives. This also happens to be one of my daughter's gifts!

The gift of mercy (also my husband's gift) is the Spirit-given ability to feel empathy and compassion for Christians and non-Christians alike. The person with this gift will be characterized by kindness and a very soft heart (again, my husband!).

Now I know this hasn't been an exhaustive study on the gifts, and I know that I've spoken of them in a somewhat random order (sorry!), but I hope you have gleaned something. Maybe you have even finally identified what some of your own gifts are.

One of the best ways to identify your gifts is by taking account of what you enjoy doing and even what you feel compelled to do. Are you compelled to give? Then you very likely have the gift of giving. Are you a study-aholic? Then you may very well have the gift of teaching.

Another thing is to notice what other people in the body ask you to do. Are you asked to help organize a brunch? Maybe it has been observed that you have the gift of administrations. And never rule out what other people actually say they see your gifts to be. Many times other people identify our gifts before we do.

And here are some examples of how to use your gifts as you begin to realize what they are:

- ✝ Do you have a good singing voice? You could have the gift of leading others into worship.

✝ Do you have a heart for prayer? Most churches have groups that meet each week for intercessory prayer—that is praying for the needs of the church, the country, the pastors and leaders of the church, and others who are in need of prayer. And watch those God brings into your life on a personal level. Could it be that He is asking you to take time out of your schedule to intercede for them?

✝ Do you have the gift of teaching? I don't know of a church on earth that doesn't need teachers in the Sunday school program, as well as for the children of the moms who are attending Bible study each week. And what about having a Bible study in your home and leading others in a study of the Word?

I want to interject a note here. I think that many times when a person feels they have the gift of teaching, they hold out and wait until God gives them one of the key places of teaching in their church. Now from my experience, there aren't that many of these positions available; but there is always room for teachers in some of the places I have already mentioned. Don't hold out—if you have the gift use it! And then, as you are faithful in a small thing (not that teaching children is a small thing—in fact it is probably the bigger thing!), God will give you more.

✝ Do you have the gift of mercy? Guess what—you can use this gift everywhere you go! And there are also great opportunities at your church in ministries like the convalescent ministry and the prison ministry.

✝ Do you have the gift of exhortation? Then God will give you opportunities with those you already know—to encourage them when they doubt, and from time to time to exhort them to keep the faith and live godly lives. And, again, as an exhorter, you may even be called on to teach.

Early in my walk, I took a test on the spiritual gifts which made me aware of the fact that I did not have the gift of teaching. But it also showed me that I was really strong (ten out of ten) in exhortation. Now I would never have thought that I could be used as a teacher—and in fact, when I was first called to pray about teaching that thought came to me loud and clear—you don't have this gift! But when I had done that test a few years earlier, I remembered reading a paragraph of explanation on the gift of exhortation that said that often exhorters made good teachers. I can't begin to tell you how much that little sentence helped me when I realized that God was, indeed, calling me to teach. It was my fall-back thought. Yes, it's true, I don't have the gift of teaching ... but I do have the gift of exhortation.

The funny thing is that many years later, after teaching and also leading a large Bible study, I did a test like that again. This time, not only did I score much higher in teaching but I scored lower in exhortation! And, when previously I had scored low in administrations, now my score was much higher there. I began to realize that our capabilities increase as we use a particular gift. I hope this thought is encouraging to you!

- ✣ Do you have the gift of evangelism? Many churches have street witnessing teams that go out on a weekly basis to minister to those who don't know Christ. And the Harvest Crusades are also a wonderful avenue for your gift.

There are so many ways to use your gifts! I remember it used to seem like if you weren't a group leader in the Bible study, you weren't using your gifts. It seemed like that was the spot everyone wanted. But what if your gift isn't leadership? Then what??? Then the formula doesn't work.

Some people don't have the gift of leadership. They have other gifts. Many of the most beautiful gifts are ones that aren't necessarily seen (or noticed) by others—like interceding, giving, and helping. The bottom line really is, each of us has at least one gift, and if you want God to use you—you can be sure He will!

CHAPTER 6
Be Prepared

"I ... entreat you to walk in a manner worthy of the calling with which
you have been called."
Ephesians 4:1

I had the opportunity one year to speak at my church at a leadership conference on the theme of *walking in the light*. As I considered the theme, the Lord immediately brought Ephesians 4:1 to my mind, where Paul calls us to walk worthy of our calling. Now, in the strictest sense, that verse speaks to the calling we have as Christians—but I think of it this way: If every Christian is called to walk in the light—or walk in a worthy manner—how much more those who have been called into ministry.

When I first stepped into ministry at Harvest Christian Fellowship, I was serving in the women's Bible study as a group leader. As we finished the study that year and entered into summer vacation, I was asked to pray about being a senior leader the following year. I remember immediately realizing that this was an important thing for me—I needed to hear from the Lord on it. So, I prayed and sought the Lord, and He assured me that He was calling me to this new position. So, very humbly, and with the realization of the importance of my new position, I stepped out and said yes.

That summer, before the new year of Bible study began, there happened to be a big worship event in Costa Mesa. My husband and I decided to go and we went with another leader in the Bible study and her husband. Well, we were having a fun time! This particular leader was a fun-loving person and so was my husband, and so, as the evening proceeded, they began to have some fun. They happened to be sitting next to each other and so they began to make little jokes. They were funny—I have to admit—but I began very quickly to become uncomfortable. I remember having the distinct thought that there were other ladies there that might be under my leadership in the upcoming year of Bible study. I had the inherent sense that I needed to be an example to them. In fact, I *wanted* to be an example to them! So I asked them, fairly strongly, to please stop their joking, which was escalating by the minute, and finally they did.

After the event, as we were leaving, the other leader turned to me and she said, "Oh Linda, take off the mask." To which I replied, "I'm not wearing a mask." Because I wasn't! In fact, her words made me realize that very thing. I wasn't wearing a mask. That was who I was.

I remember another day, years ago, when my friend Jan was teaching at the Harvest women's Bible study. She said something that day I have never forgotten—just one of those very simple things that the Lord often uses to speak to me. She said that every day when her son David would leave for school or, I imagine, anywhere else he would leave the house for, there was something she would always say to him. She would say, "David, *remember who you are.*"

I love that. Remember who you are. In other words, when you walk out of this house, David, remember who you are *and act accordingly.* I think that's what I was doing that night at the worship event. I was remembering who I was. I was considering the high calling that God had placed on my life, and the example I was to others.

In this chapter, I want to ask you to consider these two things:
- ✢ Are you careful to remember who you are?
- ✢ Have you considered the high calling with which you have been called?

You know, before people are called into positions of ministry, unbeknownst to them, they are being watched. In Bible study, we had a very distinct pattern that we would follow every year:

- ✤ At the end of the summer, before the new year of Bible study began, we would have a training day for the leaders: returning leaders, new leaders, all leaders.
- ✤ During the year we had leaders' meetings each month to encourage and help the leaders through their year of ministry.
- ✤ As the Bible study year began to come to a close, I would ask the leaders to begin to pray for the next year of study—whether or not the Lord would be calling them to serve again.
- ✤ At that same time, the leaders were to be looking at their groups for women they felt would qualify to be new leaders the following year.

So, every year in March I would devote an entire leaders' meeting to the subject of *looking for new leaders.* At that meeting, we would talk about what kinds of things they should be looking for as they considered whether or not the Lord might be calling one of their ladies into the ministry. I actually had a form listing the things the leader was to consider about her women—very simple things—qualities that were simple and basic, but extremely important to me when I was bringing someone new into the ministry.

As I was considering what the Lord would have me share with you about *your* personal preparation for ministry, I thought about that list—that very simple list of very simple character qualities that are crucial in a spiritual leader.

As I go over this list, which is actually a questionnaire, I'd like you to consider whether or not—if you had been in my group—you would have been someone I would have recommended for leadership.

1) Are you a born-again Christian—do you have a *personal* relationship with Jesus Christ?

Of course this is basic. The only way you and I can do spiritual work is to be alive spiritually. This is "Choosing Leadership 101"!

2) Do you display faith and dependence on God?

Do you struggle every time you come to a trial in your life? Do you cry and complain and tell everyone your troubles? Stop it! Discipline yourself to trust God. Sometimes it is just that simple! Decide that you're going to believe God for the problem and watch and see what He will do! I remember one day coming to a situation that looked immediately bad. I decided right off the bat that I was not going to be troubled! I prayed to the Lord and said, "Lord, You knew this was going to happen. You must have something much better for us, and so I'm just going to trust you." (I always laugh when I say, "I'm *just* going to trust You, God. Isn't that the silliest?) Now the problem wasn't worked out immediately, and it created some difficult situations for a time—but it did get worked out—and not any faster, I imagine, than if I had fretted over it. And there are benefits to the way it worked out. You see, we can trust God. Period. And people notice when we trust God. People will see your faith and realize that there is *just something about you!*

3) Are you well grounded in basic, foundational truths of the Word?

You don't need to be a Bible scholar to serve the Lord—but you do need to have a basic understanding of the truths of the Bible. The Lord spoke to me many years ago, before I stepped one foot into formal ministry, and showed me that a new Christian can lead another person to Christ—you see they can share with them the exact message they just heard! But only a mature Christian can lead others to maturity. You need to be rooted and grounded in the truths of God's Word in order to help bring others closer to Him.

4) Do you display discipline in your life? Are your priorities in order?

I had a leader years ago get up and share at the year-end leaders' luncheon that she had always had a problem with being consistent. She'd start things, but not finish them. That year, when she was called to be a group leader, she determined that she was going to be consistent in her attendance. At the end of the year she was able to share with our whole group that she had been there *consistently*! It was a victory for her. And I believe that just by disciplining herself in that one area, she probably gained in other areas, as well. That seems to be the way the Lord does it!

5) Are you dependable?

My friend Patty used to say it this way: If you say you're going to bring potatoes to the brunch, do you bring them? I could never bring someone into a position of leadership that I wasn't sure I could depend on.

6) Are you willing to take on responsibility?

You will never find a position in ministry that doesn't require you to be responsible—and *very* responsible, at that. If this is a problem, start working on it now.

7) Are you courteous, kind, and tactful?

It is very difficult to give someone a position of leadership who doesn't have these qualities. It is part of being a woman of good reputation. And I want to add here—this isn't limited to how you behave in church. How are you on the soccer field, or at your children's baseball games? It all counts! It all reveals who you are.

8) Are you easy to approach?

Do people feel comfortable with you? Almost every position of ministry will require you to be around people! If you think this might be a problem area for you (maybe you've always had trouble making friends or talking to people), then begin to pray and ask God to show you what you can to do to make a difference. You might even ask your closest and safest friend for help in this area.

9) Are you a person of prayer?

Praying with people really gives us an inside channel to where they are spiritually. You may not be able to pray long and eloquent prayers (and that's not necessarily a bad thing!), but can you talk to God? Do you talk to God? It's vitally important to anyone in ministry that they have a good prayer life. Believe me, when you are given those responsibilities we've already talked about, you'll need to talk to Him a lot!

10) Are you able to submit yourself to authority?

Very important in ministry. Vitally important, actually. You *will* have someone over you. They *will* be making decisions. You may not like their decisions. If you feel God has called you to that place of ministry, you will need to submit yourself to the decisions of your authority and display a willingness to do so—even if you think they are wrong! You let God handle that.

11) Are you ambitious?

I will be honest with you; I never called someone into leadership who seemed ambitious (striving for position). Remember what Sanders says, "The true spiritual leader will never canvass for promotion."[1] I love that! And I believe it's true. If you have a problem with ambition—lay it down right now, and work at making your character ready so that God can call you at the appointed time.

12) Are you dominant with your own ideas?

This goes along with submission. You can have ideas. In fact, you probably have great ones. And there may come a day when everything you suggest is taken to heart and acted upon. But I can pretty much guarantee that when you first step into your position, you will share your thoughts and there will be smiles and nods, but most of them will not be acted upon. I think this is the part where we earn our stripes. After a while, when you have become more grounded in your position, you'll be given more freedom and get to act on at least *some* of your great ideas!

13) Do you respond well to constructive suggestions?

This is such a hard one, but it's so important. And it really shows where you are spiritually. This could be a "make it or break it" for you. If this is hard, pray! And then, when you're given the opportunity to prove yourself here (which you will!), bite your lip if you must, go home and ask God to help you see how He wants you to apply what you were told.

14) Can you keep a confidence?

Another important integrity test. The next time you get a chance—practice! Zip your lip.

15) Are you able to give yourself fully to the commitment which is required for the ministry?

If you were called today to be in that position you have dreamt of—would you be able to fully commit yourself to whatever it entailed? Don't ever say yes to a position of ministry *hoping* that you'll be able to commit to it. Now we all step into ministry hoping that we'll be able *to do the job*—because we are usually called to do something that we can't do in ourselves. We need God! But we shouldn't say yes unless we are ready to give the time that is required for the job to be done. Are you being asked to work one morning a week in the Children's ministry for a year? Count the cost. If you know you can't commit, don't say yes. Pray—God will show you. Ask Him for a Scripture that shows you His thoughts on the matter. If He says you can do it—then you can.

16) Is your family supportive?

I hate to hear anyone say that their family is jealous of the time they give to the Lord. That just shouldn't happen. My friend who defined dependability with "potatoes" had another great idea. She had a very high position of ministry—one that was very time-consuming. She said that every year when she was asked to make her commitment for the following year of ministry, she sat down with her husband and children and asked them for their input. What a great thing to do! In fact, by doing this you are actually giving them some investment in the work you are doing for the Lord.

On the other side of the coin, I always told those I was considering for leadership that if their husband said no, then the answer was no. That's hard—but it's right. It has to do with priorities. If this is the case for you—pray and ask God to soften his heart. You'll never know the volumes it will speak to him if you ask him and he says no and, consequently, you turn the position down. You will have just given him respect and authority. That could be the very thing that changes his mind!

17) Do you have a servant's heart?

Next to being born again, this may be the most important ingredient in being prepared to serve. Scripture tells us that "even the Son of Man did not come to be served, but to serve, and to give His life a ransom for many" (Mark 10:45). You will more than likely never be called to give your life for the ministry, but you should resemble your Savior by being a servant. It should be the highest compliment to hear someone say that you have a servant's heart.

18) Are you filled and empowered with the Holy Spirit?

This is essential for doing God's work. Otherwise, you'll be doing it in the flesh, and I guarantee you, you'll burn out. Ephesians 5:18 teaches us that we need to *be being filled*—in other words, we need to be filled on a daily basis! I know I do. I never want to minister in my flesh—it bears no fruit, and it's a waste of time for everyone involved. Ask God to fill you and empower you with His Spirit. He will! Ask Him to lead you by His Spirit. He will!

This is the perfect opportunity to take stock of your life. Is there an area in which you aren't quite there? Begin to ask God to help you in that area! And believe me—He will!

CHAPTER 7
Just Say Please

"Do for others what you would like them to do for you."
Matthew 7:12 NLT

One day while talking to my friend Shauna about different aspects of ministry, I made the comment that I think we need to train our women to exhibit good etiquette in ministry. She said to me: "That sounds like a chapter in a book." So—here it is!

There are myriad things we could talk about in this chapter, but I'm just going to address a few. Unfortunately, my examples will probably come most often from the negative. I think that's when we see the lack of etiquette the clearest. And they will often have to do with teaching, since that is what I do. I'm sorry if I offend anyone in this chapter. I truly don't intend to. But I hope to bring to light some things that I think might make a difference.

Managing your time—as a person in the ministry of the Lord, it is important that you take care to make sure that everyone who is ministering gets their chance. We can think that our part is so important that we forget that everyone else's part is important too! During our morning of Bible study, the administrator got up and gave a small devotional thought and then followed with the announcements; the worship team led the group in worship; the teacher gave the message;

the group leader led the group time; and the women in the group shared their answers from the lessons they had worked on that week. Who had the most important part of the morning? Everyone did! We need to remember that.

If you are given ten minutes, take ten minutes. If you are given 40 minutes, take 40 minutes. Of course you can't always be perfect with this, but do your best to manage your time so that everyone gets the time that has been allotted to them.

Fulfilling the commitment you make to the ministry—ministry is hard; much harder, I expect, than we realize when going into it. And yet, when we know that we've been called by the Lord, we not only know that He will enable us to do the job but that He will enable us to complete the work we have begun.

I believe it is very rare that the Lord calls us to do something and then calls us out before it is finished. Not that it *never* happens—it is possible that He might call us out early, but that is the rare occasion.

We must realize when we make our commitment that there are many people who are depending on us to finish it. Don't make the commitment until you have God's mind on it. Once you've made it, trust Him to enable you to complete it, regardless of the circumstances. I believe He will reward you when you look past your difficult situation and do what you said you would do.

Fulfilling each of the requirements that go along with your area of ministry—I've had many well-intended women who said a hearty "yes" when asked to be a part of the ministry, but who actually only fulfilled a portion of what they were asked to do. There are many facets to the ministry. For a group leader or a substitute leader of a Bible study, the obvious thing is that they will do their lesson, prepare their lesson in order to lead the group, be there for the group time, and lead the group. But there are several behind-the-scenes facets to the ministry as well. When I oversaw the Bible study, the leaders were to be at the church early for prayer, before the study began. They were to plan and be prepared to lead what we called "Koinonias"—a time of fellowship that we had every month or so, in place of the study. They had to attend the monthly leaders' meetings. All of these things were mandatory and were fully explained to them *before* they said yes to the ministry. And yet from time to time, I would have a leader who only did the most obvious parts of the ministry; and that was always a problem for me as her leader.

Usually the person who didn't get to the prayer time had a good reason—the only problem was that she had a good reason week after week. Usually the leader who couldn't make it to the leaders' meeting had a good reason—the only problem was that she had a good reason month after month. Eventually, I would have to sit down with her and talk through the commitment she had made to the ministry. In fact, I ended up putting together a ministry form that carefully listed each aspect of the ministry:

- ✣ I will be there for prayer time each morning of study.
- ✣ I will attend each of the monthly leaders' meetings.
- ✣ I will have my lesson completed and prepared for group time.
- ✣ I will prepare for each Koinonia, etc.

Before the ladies gave their answers for the ministry each year, we would go over that list. I would say to them, "If there's anything on this list that you can't say 'yes' to, then it is more than likely that you are not being called to this ministry." You see, those things were mandatory. I would tell them things like—"Don't make a dentist appointment for the morning of Bible study or the day of the leaders' meeting. Be sure to have your lessons prepared the night before the study, so you can be there on time. Try to have your clothing picked out, so that you won't have any last minute problems the morning of study. Set your alarm! Get up on time!" In other words, my message was, "Be prepared!"

Of course things come up from time to time. That's not the point here. But when things come up *often* and *regularly*, then I have to question whether or not the person is fully committed to the ministry they said yes to—or even if they were truly called by the Lord, in the first place.

If you say yes to a position of ministry, then be prepared to do each and every part of what that ministry requires. If you find that you are constantly having excuses—even good excuses—for not fulfilling all the facets of your ministry, you should go to your leader and talk it over with her. Don't make her come to you. You go to her and ask for her help. If God has truly called you, then He will enable you to do everything you've said yes to.

Teaching the chapter you're assigned—if you have ever taught a message and then the next week the teacher got up and taught your chapter over again, then you will already know why this is a problem! The reverse can be true, as well. Maybe you're lined up to teach Romans 2 and the speaker the week before you (the Romans 1 teacher) goes into your chapter and points out all the good stuff. There's really no need to do this. All God's Word is exciting and meaningful. Really, if you do this, it's probably because you have a pet teaching in the passage you're using, instead of being diligent to teach the chapter you've been assigned. Believe me, if God wants you to share the thing that is so dear to your heart, He'll give you the opportunity!

This could also happen at a retreat, a brunch, or any another occasion where a series of messages are given. Be very careful to keep within the boundaries of your topic. If I ever feel that I need to move into someone else's territory (sometimes the boundaries are not clear-cut), I make sure to ask if I'll be stepping on their toes. It's good etiquette!

Finishing or adding to the message of someone who has just spoken—I've had this happen more than once! And I can tell you that it usually ends up being something that takes away the impact that I was hoping to impart. On one occasion, I was giving a message that I hoped would lift the weight off the women in regard to working to earn what Christ has freely given us. The main thing I was hoping my forty-five minutes of sharing would produce was free women. When I got done, someone very important to the women got up and sort of concluded the evening by adding her thoughts to what I had said. She didn't disagree with what I said, she just elaborated, which was fine, and it was her right to do so; but by the time she got done, I must tell you, somehow she had put back on the women's shoulders everything I had tried to take off!

Sometimes you may be in a Bible study setting where people are encouraged (or desire and are allowed) to get up and add something that is on their heart.

Now, I have nothing against women sharing. And in a Bible study setting, that is precisely what their group-time is for. They should have ample time in their group to share what the Lord has been showing them as they have done their study that week. But one week a woman raised her hand *while* I was teaching. I wasn't sure what to do. That hadn't happened to me before. (Actually, now that I think of it, it had—but that's another story!) So finally I said something like, "Yes, can I help you?" Or, "Yes, do you have a question?" She said she had something very important to share, and she felt like she should share it with the whole group. I said something like, "Maybe you could share that with your group during the group-time."

Now the woman who headed up the Bible study had never had anything like that happen before, and a woman came over to her (while I was still teaching, by the way—another etiquette no-no!) and told her that she felt the woman should be given a chance to share. My dear friend wasn't sure what to do. It is always a hard situation when you have to make that split-second decision, and so she said that she could get up and share after I ended my message. Well the girl began to share. At first I thought what she had to say was good, but it went on and on. All of a sudden, I had the distinct realization (I'm sure from the Holy Spirit) that what was happening was that she had just distracted the ladies from the message the Lord had for them that morning.

Now I want to emphasize again, I think the women need and deserve a right to share what the Lord is showing them and what He is doing in their lives. But we need to be careful to maintain the protectiveness of the message as best we can. I know I'm not the only one who has had this experience. I remember thinking at first that it was fine, but I truly believe the Holy Spirit showed me what was really happening. And, instead of the women going to their groups that day with the message of God on their hearts, they were caught up in what turned out to be an emotional and very me-oriented word of personal sharing. We need to be careful to guard the time that the Lord has set aside for the Word to go forth. It is an extremely important aspect of the Bible-study setting.

Approaching a speaker and speaking with her during the message time—about anything!—let's say there is a lull in the message—maybe there is a time of singing, or communion is served, or something of that nature, and while the speaker is sitting, waiting for her time to approach the pulpit again, someone approaches her and begins to ask her questions, or instruct her on what she should do at that time. These are things that are very distracting to the teacher/speaker and to the flow of the Holy Spirit. I think if we would revere the time that is set aside for the Word of God to be spoken, these kinds of things wouldn't take place.

Talking during a message—okay, I admit it, I have been a culprit here. There are often things you want to say to the one sitting next to you about a point that is being made. And to a degree, I think that's alright. But don't start asking your friend where she wants to go for lunch. Not only are you not listening at this point—but now she can't listen either! And on the same note, try not to start making grocery lists, etc., during a message. You never know what God might have had for you that morning that you missed because you were talking or doodling. And as a leader, not only should you *not* be talking during the message—but, because you are an example to those around you, you should be listening intently *and* taking notes.

I remember years ago at Bible study there were a few leaders who always sat in the very front row. I asked them once why they always sat up front and they said they didn't want to miss *one* word of the message that was being spoken. What a great reverence for God's Word they had and what a great example they were to the women in their groups! In fact, as I think of them, I now recall that many of the leaders who eventually went on to greater places of spiritual ministry were among those who were found, week after week, in the front of the sanctuary.

Talking on your cell phone in any formal church setting—in fact, when you get to church, or someone's home, or wherever you're going for your meeting, be courteous and turn your cell-phone off! (My daughter, who is a hair-stylist, suggested that I add "when you are under the shampoo bowl" to my list!) Again, this is good etiquette for everyone—how much more important for a leader.

Let's turn this around now and look at it from the positive. We're going to call these the "Bs" of good etiquette. Here are some things that as leaders we need to *be*.

Be balanced—now I realize that I am taking a chance here of undoing everything I said earlier about being fully committed to the ministry God is calling you to. That still stands! But I want to balance what I said there with these thoughts:

I noticed over my years in ministry that it was not uncommon for women to think of their ministry as being *too* important. I saw signs of this from the very early stages of my ministry. Again, since my ministry was predominantly with women's Bible study that is the area I'm thinking of here.

There were certain women (many of them) who had the tendency to think of their position in ministry as *everything*. Their whole world began to revolve around it. If anything went wrong there, they would be devastated. Now again, I believe that the ministry is very important. And I believe that if you feel God is calling you to a certain position, then you need to do what it takes to fulfill your ministry. But it is not your life. It is a *part* of your life—and a great one at that! But it is not your life.

Your family is always your first priority. Your husband comes before your ministry. Your children come before your ministry. Managing your home comes before your ministry. In fact, Paul told Timothy that when he was appointing elders in the church, this was something he was to look for. A person's home had to be in order. (See 1 Timothy 3:4-5.)

If God is truly calling you—which continues to be the number one thing that you need to know when stepping into ministry—then He will enable you to put your family and your home first and still be able to fulfill your ministry.

Be on time—whether it is to Bible study, a prayer meeting, a retreat, or just lunch with friends, endeavor to be a timely person. When you arrive late, you are a distraction to the others who are gathered and listening or participating. And as a leader, you, above all, should be on time.

Be prepared—when you get to the church or the meeting place, have your preparations completed in order to fulfill your ministry role. Don't sit in the back and finish preparing your lesson. Those in your group will see you and it will send a bad message. Arrive with your lesson done. Arrive with your message finished. Arrive with your casserole in hand.

Be courageous—this may not exactly be considered *etiquette*—but it's important. Do what you've been called upon to do, with your eyes on the Lord. I loved something I read in *Spiritual Leadership* many years ago (it really helped me). Speaking of courage, it said, "The highest degree of courage is seen in the person who is most fearful but refuses to capitulate to it."[1]

Be compassionate—listen to what those around you are saying. Encourage them. Care for your little sheep. When there is a ministry situation that calls for confrontation, remember to speak the truth in love (see Ephesians 4:15).

Be a good communicator—when you are in any position of leadership, communication is important. You need to be communicative to those you are working with, those you are working under, and those you are leading. This is an especially important requirement when you have others who are subordinate to your leadership. If you are in that kind of position—take note: The only way they will know what you are thinking is if you tell them. The only way you will know what they are thinking is if you take the time and listen to them. They may have great ideas that you can avail yourself of. They may have problems that you don't realize. They may just need encouragement.

I don't know if anyone else has had this experience, but as a married woman I can tell you that my husband and I worked best together when we were communicating. When we stopped talking, we had a bad habit of getting irritable with each other. We might have misunderstood each others' meanings or motives. We simply worked best together when we had a good and healthy flow of communication. The same is true in ministry. When we stop talking to each other it gives the enemy room to work. Be careful of this.

Be polite—remember the Golden Rule: "Do for others what you would like them to do for you" (Matthew 7:12 NLT). When you ask someone to do something for you, remember to say "please."

Be thankful—has someone used their spiritual gifts to help you? Thank them. Haven't you noticed how much quicker you are to help the one who is thankful? Thankfulness goes a long way. Sometimes in ministry we expect everyone to do their jobs, but forget to let them know that they are appreciated. Be sure to do this.

Be sorry—have you hurt someone? Tell him or her you're sorry. If you realize that there is something between you and another leader, call her and ask if you have offended her in some way. If you have, be sorry. (See Matthew 5:23-24.) Like thankfulness, sincere apologies go a long way!

Be an example—anyone who knows me knows that I love Oswald Chambers. I have been reading his devotion, *My Utmost for His Highest*, for over 35 years now! And I can truly say that I have drunk deeply of his spirit. In fact, I consider him my spiritual mentor. His thoughts on the Word of God and on spiritual things have helped to create and form much of my perspective.

I want to share a statement he made about leadership which I feel is in keeping with this theme. He says, "The viewpoint of a worker for God must not be as near the highest as he can get, it must be the highest. Be careful to maintain strenuously God's point of view, it has to be done every day, bit by bit ..."[2]

When I was a fairly new Christian, I was given a little card that had my name at the top of it with the meaning of my name and a special verse under it. The verse was Psalm 29:1-2:

> "Ascribe to the Lord, O sons of the mighty,
> Ascribe to the Lord glory and strength.
> Ascribe to the Lord the glory due His name;
> Worship the Lord in holy array"

At that time of my fairly new walk with the Lord, I remember stopping a little on that last line—*worship the Lord in holy array*.

I was very young at the time, and to be really honest with you, I wasn't sure I wanted to take that part of the verse on. I kind of wanted my freedom in the area of how I was arrayed! I remember even looking that verse up and studying it a little and, sure enough, I was happy to find out that, in the truest sense, it wasn't talking about *my* holiness (or my dress!) but His. But the Lord still challenged me on that one.

There was this little top that I liked to wear—it was quite comfortable and I liked the way I looked in it! (I'm being really honest here—this was when I was still in my 20s!) Now, although it was the 70s, I believe the top I am thinking about is popular again today. (I'm not going to say any more about it!)

For a while I felt a sort of conviction about wearing that top. But I would always think—it's alright, there's nothing wrong with it. And I would justify that people wore things that were a lot worse! But there was always this little nagging inside about it.

One day, I was kneeling beside my bed praying, and the thought of that stupid top came to my mind. I thought—*oh that's no big deal*—and I tried to get back to prayer—but I couldn't pray. I absolutely hit a wall. I couldn't move forward. I realized very quickly that it was that stupid top!!! And that was all it took. I got up off my knees, took that top out of my drawer, and put it in a bag of things to go to the Goodwill. It was over. I went back to my knees and spent time in the presence of the Lord.

Evidently it wasn't "no big deal" after all. To the Lord, it seemed to be a very big deal! Now that doesn't mean that I didn't see other Christians dressed similarly—but for me God said, "no."

I didn't realize it then, but God was in the process of calling me into ministry. I believe that was part of the preparation, because the ministry He was calling me to would require that I be an example to others. Only the Lord knows what would have happened to me and to my future ministry if I had refused that one thing. How amazingly ridiculous it would have been to jeopardize the calling He had on my life because of one silly top!

You know, just as there is a *spiritual* cost to ministry, there is a *practical* cost, as well. We must remember whom we are serving—we are serving the Most High God. We need to be sure that we look and act like it.

I remember a wonderful story I read about Amy Carmichael that really made an impression on me. While she was a missionary in Japan, she had gone to minister to a woman who was quite ill. As she spoke about the Savior, the woman seemed to be at the point of turning to Christ when she suddenly noticed and was distracted by Amy's fur gloves. And this is what Amy says: "I went home, took off my English clothes, put on my Japanese Kimono, and never again, I trust, risked so very much for the sake of so very little."[3]

The question to us is, how much are we willing to risk to dress the way of the world?

Paul's word on the subject is this: "Likewise, I want women to adorn themselves with proper clothing, modestly and discreetly, not with braided hair and gold or pearls or costly garments; but rather *by means of good works, as befits women making a claim to godliness*" (1 Timothy 2:9, emphasis added).

I know there is so much more to be said on good etiquette in ministry, and I'm sure I have only touched the tip of the iceberg. I trust the Lord will use these thoughts to speak to you in the possibility that you are risking something very great for the sake of something very little.

CHAPTER 8
Take the Lead

"If you are a leader, exert yourself to lead."
Romans 12:8 (NEB)

If you have been called to take a position of leadership, then others will be following *your* lead. You'll be the responsible one, you'll be the one everyone is looking to—do you feel able? Probably not. But if God has called you, then you will be.

Because you are the one *called*, you are the one who will be given the spiritual power and ability to do the job. If you don't take the lead, either nobody will or someone else will—but it will be someone who has not been given the spiritual enabling.

The Holy Spirit's enabling is given to the one called by God, no matter what they feel like or what they think about themselves. The power and ability to lead in your particular position will not be given to anybody but you. So you must be willing to take the lead!

Some of the dictionary's definitions for the word *lead* are as follows:

- ✢ "To go with or ahead of so as to show the way; guide."
- ✢ "To cause to progress by or as pulling or holding: to lead a child by the hand."
- ✢ "To serve as or indicate a route for …" (My example—being a pointer or pointing the way to the Lord.)

- ✠ "To control the actions or affairs of; direct."
- ✠ "To influence the ideas, conduct, or actions of."
- ✠ "To be first among."
- ✠ "To be the principle participant in: to lead a discussion."
- ✠ "To have control or command."[1]

All of these definitions are good, and would be beneficial to ponder. But the final meaning I mentioned—to have control or command—may be the best for the focus we are taking here, that of *taking the lead*.

Leader (by dictionary definition) means: "One who or that which goes ahead or in advance. One who acts as a guiding force, commander, etc."[2]

Leadership means: "The office, position, or capacity of a leader; guidance. Ability to lead, exert authority, etc."[3]

So, to *lead* is to have control or command, to be a *leader* is to act as a guiding force—a commander, and *leadership* is the ability to lead and to exert authority. We also know that leadership is servanthood, as taught by Christ Himself in Mark 10.

Do you remember I shared with you the great statement made in the book *Spiritual Leadership* about the fact that term *leader* occurs only six times in the KJV—and that it is usually referred to in different terms, the most prominent being *servant*?

I like that statement because it makes it very clear that leadership is servanthood and, if we are going to get off balance, let's be sure we do it in that direction—to err on the side of servant, not commander!

But I want to lean on the *commander* side just long enough to make certain that we get the point that every ministry needs a leader and if you have been called to be that leader, then you need to step up to the plate and exert yourself to lead.

I've written down a few things that I believe can keep us from being effective leaders:

1. Becoming too familiar with those you have been placed over in leadership.

Let's just say you are a Bible-study group leader. You are not called to be best friends with the ladies in your group. They don't need a best friend in you—they need a leader! They need someone they can look to for spiritual guidance and encouragement and they need to have respect for you in the sense of your position as their leader.

If you become too familiar with those you are leading, if they know too much about you and you know too much about them, you are likely to find your ability to minister to them affected.

Does that mean that you can't be friendly and close and caring? Of course not! In fact, if you aren't those things you aren't a good leader. But your followers need to see you as someone separate. Someone set apart. Not just one of the gang.

The Lord will give you people with whom you can share your daily life. You will have your own close friends. And there may be someone that will *become* your close friend as the years progress—this happens all the time.

But for the time being, those God has placed under your care need to see you as someone separate from themselves—someone that God has placed over them and who has His authority and His ability to minister to them.

You will not care for or love your flock any less by allowing for that separation. The truth is, it is actually easier to get too familiar than it is to allow that separation and be the leader. Be careful of your position. Guard it!

Another point here—you are their leader—not their mother hen. I have seen leaders get burdened and burned out when they have taken on more than God has asked them to as a leader.

You are not expected to help those under you through their daily lives. You may (and probably will) have people that will look to you for that. You love them, you care for them, you sincerely pray for them, and you *keep them directed to the Lord*—who is the one who *can* help them.

If you begin to feel that the load is too heavy, check and see if you have taken on more than God has asked. He'll only give you the strength to carry what He has given you.

2. Allowing someone with a strong personality to take over the lead.

Some of you are stronger and more aggressive by nature and can easily take control of the situation. Some of you are quieter and more reserved by nature. You needn't do anything to change who you are— God called you to be the leader exactly as you are. But if you are of a quieter nature, then you might need to be careful of this.

It can especially be a problem when you have someone under your lead who feels very adequate and maybe even more qualified than you to take the lead. And maybe they are—but God has chosen you. If you find you have a problem in this area, share your situation with the one in authority over you so that they can pray for you and give you direction.

But take heed to this—if once you relinquish your leadership to someone else, it will be very difficult to get it back. It must be evident that you are the leader and that you are the one in control. There may be an uncomfortable moment or two, but you must maintain your leadership position at all costs.

Remember, God has not given your leadership position to anyone else—not even the wisest and most mature person under you. You are the one with the spiritual power and wisdom to lead your ministry. You are the one God is going to speak to and direct. You must not let your position of authority go!

3. Ineffective use of your time.

When you take a position of leadership, you will have to begin to make choices. Choices as to what you're going to give your strength to. If you step into your new position with the thought that nothing will really change, you can do everything you did before, it will all work out—I'm sorry to have to tell you, but you will probably find out very soon that you are mistaken.

What a great privilege it is to say, "God has called me into the ministry." You are set apart by those very words! But, by those very words you are also called to a higher standard of the use of your time and even your life. Spiritual ministry is the highest calling. Be careful that you don't allow it to be just another thing that you do during the week. Value it. Prize it. Honor it, and God will honor you!

4. Perfectionism.

Perfectionism is such a subtle danger because *it just seems so right*. I want to do everything *just* right. I want to do every perfectly! It's a trap that probably every one of us will fall into from time to time, especially those of us who are by nature perfectionists.

The bottom line that you need to remember is that God called you to your position so that *He* could work through you to minister to others.

The most perfect thing that you can offer to God is *yourself* as a living and holy sacrifice—an empty vessel for Him to fill.

We all want to be good leaders—and that's a good thing. But, if you begin by thinking that you *can't* do anything wrong, and you *mustn't* make a mistake, you're setting yourself up for a fall because you *will* do something wrong and you *will* make some mistakes. Yes, you will do your best but you are not perfect and you will not be the first perfect leader!

Perfectionism is a trap that Satan will try to use to get you off the right track. The right track is:

- ✣ Do your best to fulfill your ministry
- ✣ Put your trust in God
- ✣ Keep your relationship with Him your first priority
- ✣ Allow Him to lead you and enable you to fulfill the ministry He has given you

Oswald Chamber says something good about this. He says, "When the devil puts you into an elevated place, he makes you screw your idea of holiness beyond what flesh and blood can ever bear, it is a spiritual acrobatic performance, you are just poised and dare not move ..."[4]

Have you ever felt that way—one wrong move and it's over? If you've been in leadership, I dare say you have! But listen to what he says next. He continues, " ...but when God elevates you by His grace into the heavenly places, instead of finding a pinnacle to cling to, you find a great table-land where it is easy to move."[5]

Isn't that the best? If you are trusting God for your leadership there will be freedom and breathing room. You won't get burned out and He will carry the burden.

If you're trusting yourself for your leadership, then you're on your own and you will resort to trying to be perfect instead of letting go and letting God have His way with you and your ministry.

You are not perfect, neither am I. I don't expect you to be perfect and you probably don't expect me to be. We are usually the only ones who put that expectation on ourselves. You will make mistakes. That's okay. Learn from them and they will become tools for your future usefulness to God.

Don't try to do it yourself, you'll never make it. Don't be like Martha—running around trying to make everything *just so.* Be like Mary. Sit at His feet, rest in Him, and let Him minister through you.

I thought of a couple other hindrances which I'm not going to elaborate on, but I'm just going to throw out for you to think over—*popularity* and *ambition*.

Beware of seeking popularity and being ambitious. If you see yourself looking for popularity or motivated by ambition, stop yourself at once and work against these fleshly motivations. They are natural motivations, but they are not from God. And both of them will side track you and cause you to be ineffective as a leader.

And just one more thing—*comparing yourself to other leaders*. Whether you compare yourself favorably or unfavorably, either way you lose. If you come out, in your estimation, as better, it will cause you to be proud. If you come out, in your estimation, as worse, it will bring you discouragement. Just be who you are and trust the Lord that He knew what He was up to when He chose you.

A missionary to the Philippines once shared with me that the Lord had taught her to lay down three things: pride, perfectionism, and performance. I think that's a good rule of thumb!

When David was charging Solomon with the work of building the temple, he said these words to him: "Be strong and courageous, and act; do not fear nor be dismayed, for the Lord God, my God, is with you. He will not fail you nor forsake you until all the work for the service of the house of the Lord is finished" (1 Chronicles 28:20).

This is God's word for you as well. If you are a leader, exert yourself to lead! You *are* a leader, so be strong and courageous and act!

CHAPTER 9

Study, Write, Speak!

"Always be prepared to give an answer to everyone who asks you to give the reason for the hope that you have."
1 Peter 3:15 NIV

What I want to do in this chapter is to speak heart to heart on the topic of sharing God's love, heart, Word, and encouragement with others. You may be called to teach children or you may be asked to do a devotion or you may be called to be a teacher at a Bible study, who knows? Maybe you are already doing these things, but would just like some encouragement. I'm going to share with you some of the things the Lord has taught me as a teacher of His Word over the years, and I'm praying there will something here that will help you in your particular place of speaking/sharing (or maybe even prepare you for what lies ahead!).

My plan is to be simple. I am simple and I like to look at things that way. Let's begin with the *study* part of the process. Because I am a teacher of God's Word, I'm going to share from that perspective. If you are doing a devotion, you probably won't have to dig quite so deep—but you *will* more than likely have a Scripture reference for your sharing, and you would want to follow these steps, or something similar to them, for your background information.

Study!

This is the nuts and bolts—this is where you're going to start. Study, with prayer, is the most important part of your preparation. To be a teacher, you must be a student. You are handling the Word of God, and that's a great responsibility!

2 Timothy 2:15 says, "Study to shew thyself approved unto God, a workman that needth not to be ashamed, rightly dividing the word of truth" (KJV).

When we begin our preparation to teach, it's always first things first—to begin with it's just you and the Word of God. Before you ever open a commentary or any other study book you want to see what the Holy Spirit is ministering to you personally.

Preliminary study—
- ✣ Read the entire book of the Bible you will be sharing from. This gives you a good sense and basic understanding of what the book is about as a whole—and that will definitely show, even if you are only sharing on a small passage in the book.

- ✣ Read the passage before and after. This helps with your understanding of the context.

- ✣ Read the passage many times using different translations for differences in wording (believe it or not, even *one word* may help you understand the meaning better). And also, for emphasis, many times I will read a verse to my audience from several translations to help *them* see it better.

Digging Deeper—
Next we begin digging—really getting into the Scripture, seeing what it has to say to us. Although I don't personally use the inductive method of study (well, I actually do, but in a round-about sort of way!), I think it will give you the best possible basis for your study and it will show you exactly what is important for you to know and present to your audience. For a really good and in-depth understanding of this method, there are many good books on the subject. Anne Graham Lotz teaches

this concept amazingly, and I owe what I understand of it to her. But, again, I'm going to present it to you in a very simplified way.

Step 1

- *Find the facts*—this is the *observation* part of the process. Ask yourself questions like: who is speaking, what is taking place, what is the main subject. List the facts and their verses.

- *Look for the heart*—this is where you look for the *spiritual meaning* or *lesson* of the passage. You may ask yourself a question like: "What spiritual truths are taught here?" You may look for a command, a word of exhortation, a promise, etc. Make a list of the lessons you get out of each verse or grouping of verses.

- *Hear Him speak*—this is where you find a *personal application* for the lessons you got in the last step. Look back over your lesson list and you might ask yourself how you will apply each lesson to yourself.

Step 2

- *Summary statement of the facts*—see if you can state the *content* of the passage in a couple of sentences. This will give you one main theme or summary statement of the passage.

This step in the process is a very important step in your studying and then in your writing. You need to know what your passage is about. Whether or not you study using the inductive method, you will need to be able to say in a sentence or two what your passage—or in other words your message—is about.

In the book *Effective Bible Teaching*, by Jim Wilhout and Leland Ryken, they speak about teaching the *big idea.* They talk about having a single focus around which the lesson (or in other words, the message) is built. They quote Haddon W. Robinson, who says that teachers need to be able to answer two questions—"What am I talking about?" and "What exactly am I saying about what I am talking about?"[1]

Although you will talk about many things in your message, they all need to relate to this central theme. The Holy Spirit will help you with this. I read this about essay writing:

> "Most essays are focused on and controlled by a single main idea that the writer wants to communicate to readers—a central theme to which all the general statements and specific information of the essay relate. This main idea, called the thesis, encompasses the writer's attitude toward the topic and purpose in writing."[2]

So we might say that we are talking about having a *thesis* or a *summary statement* of what you are going to share. You will probably communicate this thought in your introduction—it may even be your title.

Again, *Effective Bible Teaching* says, "The statement of theme is not only a point of departure; it should be a continuous presence in the lesson."[3] In other words, it should be a thread that runs through your entire message.

In fact, in a good message you'll be redundant—you'll tell them what you're going to say, say it, and then tell them what you've said! Telling them what you're going to say is your *introduction*. Saying it is the *body* of your message. Telling them what you've said is your *conclusion*.

And it all centers around that little summary sentence you came up with in Step 2 of your study! The summary sentence you came up with has to do with the *facts* of the passage—next you began to find the meaning.

✢ *Summary statement of the meaning*—see if you can state the main lesson of the passage in a single sentence. This will be the aim of your message. It will specify what you want to accomplish.

Now we have statements declaring what our passage is about factually and spiritually, and now we move on to practical application.

✢ *Summary statement of the personal application*—look for a personal application from the content of the passage. It should come from the lesson you got in the last step. The question you might ask yourself is, how you will apply the passage as a whole to yourself. At this point Anne Graham Lotz would encourage you to come up with some personal application questions for your audience to consider. You might have a personal application question to bring home each point of your message.

So ...

Step 1 of the basic inductive method is to write out the facts, interpretation, and application.

Step 2 in my simplified method is to come up with a summary statement of the *facts*—which you can use as a title, and you can use in your introduction and throughout your message; next, come up with a summary statement of the *meaning* of the passage—which gives the aim of your message and can be like a thread running throughout; and finally, come up with a summary statement of the *application* of the passage, perhaps having a personal application question for each of your major points.

Even in the simplified method I've given you, you will probably find yourself coming up with several lessons and personal applications to go along with the facts of the passage.

So that's what you get from the *first-things-first* of your study—when it's just you and your Bible!

Then you began to fill in the gaps by doing some word study, reading a Bible dictionary and other study books and commentaries. By the time you're done, you have a message brewing in your heart and you begin to write it down. That is how the inductive method of studying and writing is used. For those who are newer teachers, this is a method that would help you get your bearings and begin to learn to teach.

Now, I've already told you that I don't use the inductive method exactly—and yet I am still trying to accomplish the same things that this method is accomplishing.

- ✢ I begin by reading and reading and reading the passage. As I read—using different translations—I take notes.
- ✢ I write down the things that strike me. The first things are always the facts. What is happening, where is it happening, why is it happening, just like we did in the first phase of our inductive study.
- ✢ Then I begin to sort of "feel" the passage. Things start to speak to my heart. This is where I begin to see the spiritual meaning of the passage. I note those things that stand out to me.

Then I start to do my research:

- ✢ Word study—not every word—just the ones that strike me as important to what I am beginning to feel in my heart.
- ✢ Commentaries—although I take notes as I read commentaries, and sometimes I will quote from them, what they do for me is mainly three things:
    - ✓ They keep me on track.
    - ✓ They reveal to me if I am in error.
    - ✓ They confirm what the Holy Spirit is already showing me.

Write and Speak!

After I've spent time studying in these various ways, the time comes when I simply have to begin writing. Sometimes I don't feel ready at all. But that's where the Holy Spirit comes in! I might just write my first thoughts—maybe just beginning where the chapter begins, and then I find myself writing a message. (A good method for newer teachers is to write your message going from verse to verse.)

So I study and study and study, and then I *wait for the Spirit to move*, and then I write and write and write.

I write my messages out pretty much word for word. Some of you will not have to do that. Some of you may just use an outline with some points in between. If you do it this way, the thing you have to be careful with is your time. You need to make sure your message fits into the time slot you have been given.

Outlines—
I rarely use an outline. My brain just doesn't automatically work that way. If the Lord gives me one I use it—but I don't force one.

You will probably look for an outline and use one—it does help to keep continuity and keep your audience clear on where you are going.

One thing I want to say about outlines is to be careful about trying to be too clever. If the Lord gives you three points that all start with the same letter or rhyme or something else of that nature, that's great. But if not, just use your brain and try to be simple and clear.

Simplicity—
Keep your message simple. I love the saying, "put the cookies on the bottom shelf." You never want to speak down to people, but you do want to share a message that can be universally understood and appreciated.

There's just no reason to try to talk like a TV preacher, or to use super-big words, or to act like you are a theologian. Your audience won't be ministered to any more than they will by the *simple sharing of someone who loves Jesus*.

A good rule of thumb is this: know your material well, but keep your presentation of it simple. You may have to leave some things out to streamline your message for the sake of clarity.

There is a great temptation to say too much and to say too many things, especially for newer teachers. There is a temptation as a new teacher to try to say everything you have ever heard about the subject you're teaching. You don't have to do that! You'll probably be given many more opportunities over the years to share your heart!

Time—

You will be given a certain amount of time for your message. You need to be as careful as you are able to stay within that time limit. That care will be taken at home as you are preparing your message.

You need to realize that you're probably not the only facet of the meeting. And, although the teaching of the Word is obviously important and key to the meeting, other people will have prepared and will want to have their time as well.

You see everyone who has a job feels that their job is important—they all want the time allotted them. I have sometimes observed teachers at a Bible study go over their allotted time so far that 15 minutes of the group-time was lost. Then not only do the leaders have a more difficult time, but the students who were at home all week working on their lessons get short changed of their time to share.

You see—everyone's time is important! And everyone's part is important! You don't need to be legalistic about it—just do your best—but remember that it's good etiquette.

Refining the message—

I have to go back through my message many times before it is really ready to teach. And that is part of the writing process—getting it cleaned up. As you are writing sometimes you think something makes sense, but when you go back and read it again you realize that you haven't set the stage well enough for your point or that you've over-said the point.

So, when you finish writing your message, don't put it away and think you're through and pull it out the day you're going to teach—you'll be sorry! Give yourself enough time to go over the message several times (especially new teachers) before you have to give it.

As you go over it, you are also sort of practicing the message for when you give it. Everyone will do this differently. Do what feels right to you and what helps you the most to be ready when it's time to give it.

Content—
Now, let's look at the content of your message.

- *Introduction*—this is something you'll probably get better at as time goes by. I don't stress over this. I just begin writing my thoughts, and it seems like the Lord gives me what I need. But you may want to specifically come up with something that will capture your audience: like a question, a quotation, or a problem.

- *Body*—this is actually your message. Again, you want to find the heart, but at the same time, make sure what you center on is a central issue of the passage.

Be careful not to take a particular point (maybe a pet peeve) and go off on it. Be careful not to go on rabbit trails. Make sure you are dealing with the passage as a whole. I know I'm not the only one who has heard a preacher or a teacher share a certain pet peeve of theirs *in every message they give*. This isn't good. Don't do it.

One of the things you want to do in your message is to bridge the gap—what did it mean when it was written and what does it mean to us today? What difference does it make in my life?

- *Illustrations*—are something that you can use throughout your message to help your audience understand your points. Howard Hendricks says that illustrations are "windows that let in light, so that your hearers can say 'Aha—I see it!'"[4]

Be careful with illustrations, though. You definitely want to have some, but be careful that you don't overdo it here. You can have too many. Often the best illustrations are personal—but even in that you have to remember that *it's not about you.*

I've heard teachers who think their audience cares more about them and their personal lives than is actually the case. You don't want to waste your audiences' time telling them things that don't have a direct application to the message.

Definitely let your audience into your life. Definitely be personal. Definitely share heart to heart—but don't waste your precious allotted time (as well as your audiences' time) by telling them things that don't have a direct application to the message of the passage. They are coming to hear the Word of God!

Although I share a lot from my personal experiences, I rarely give specifics about my life. This is something the Lord has taught me. Sometimes the things I am going through are extremely personal; and I always want to be careful with my family, that I don't share something that would label them or put a negative thought in my audiences' minds. I share most often in generalities.

Now sometimes the Lord will ask you to give a specific example. If He shows you this, by the Holy Spirit, then do it. But be careful here. Your story only matters if it brings home the point of the passage.

Another way I illustrate is by quoting someone else. In fact I quote more than I illustrate.

When I do give personal illustrations, they are often just the story that tells how the Lord showed me the point I am trying to make. They're usually very simple. Often the little story that leads up to how the Lord showed me the point is my best illustration—because it personalizes the point and sort of fleshes it out.

One thing you never want to do in a personal illustration is be the hero of your story. Don't give those illustrations—let someone else do that!

So in your message you have an *introduction*, where you begin to get their attention; then you go through your points and share *information*, *explanation*, and *illustrations*, and perhaps you end each point with a *personal application* question to bring it home.

I don't always do that, although I know teachers that do and it can work well. But I think you have to be careful not to be too pat. Try to do different things to conclude your points: sometimes ask a question, sometimes you can share how God showed you the point—just be careful not to get in a rut and have a predictable message.

> ✢ *Conclusion*—to finish up your message, you want to share, in summary, what you've already said—bringing it all together.

You want your audience to be able to go home and tell someone what your message was about. The teacher talked about this, or these three things, etc. You want your message to be clear and concise enough so that people can later share what it was you said.

Practical pointers on speaking:

Handling your nerves—does the speaking part of the package scare you a little? If so, then you are in good company! Remember the Nike commercial—*Just do it!* I think that says it best!

At a *Passionate Pursuit* Conference, several years ago, Jill Briscoe was talking about *fear* and she said something that helped me so much—she said three simple words—"do it scared!"

I love that. I always feel like there's something wrong with me when I feel scared. Like that must mean I shouldn't be teaching. She said "just do it scared!" And you know what? I've done it that way many, many, many, many, many, many times!

Smile!—sometimes this is hard in the early days—just do your best. You want your audience to see that you love what you're doing. We used to say that teaching is sort of a love/hate relationship—you'll probably feel that way too. But you want your audience to see the love side.

Be careful to *speak clearly*—try your best to have your pronunciation correct—there are books for this (especially in regard to biblical names and places). Try not to speak monotonously—sometimes it's hard at first, you're just learning and you're probably petrified. Go ahead and just do your best, but work toward varying your tone and your speed and just talking to them as if they are your friends—because they really are!

Be *vulnerable*—let your audience get to know you. Let them know you're just like them. Let them know you struggle. But don't be pathetic and share *all* your troubles—in fact don't do that at all! The podium is not a place for you to share your problems—your audience has enough problems of their own.

Let them know you are a work in progress just like they are—but be careful not to share your specific struggles unless you have had a good degree of victory in that area—then it can be a praise report! But even then, be careful to be Spirit-led.

Be *excited!*—in order to get your listeners excited, you need to be excited. In order to motivate them, you need to be motivated. They need to see that you love God's Word. This is an essential pre-requisite to being a Bible teacher/speaker. And they need to see that you believe that the Bible is *infallible*. That way they can take the step of faith to believe every word in it as well.

In essence, our purpose is this:

- ✤ To help our audience construct a Christ-centered faith of their own. (If you don't have a Christ-centered faith it will show up in your teaching—you can only give them what you have.)
- ✤ To cause our audience to grow in their love for Jesus and their trust in Him.
- ✤ To challenge our audience to question where they currently are in their spiritual walk and to desire to make improvements.
- ✤ To provide our audience with words that heal and restore.

Anointing—
Don't forget that there is an anointing! 1 John 2:27 says, "And as for you, the anointing which you received from Him abides in you, and you have no need for anyone to teach you; but as His anointing teaches you about all things, and is true and is not a lie, and just as it has taught you, you abide in Him."

Trust God—
He called you, whether to speak once at a particular meeting or consistently at a weekly Bible study. If you have been called to speak on

a regular basis, look to God for scriptural confirmation of that calling. You've been asked—has He confirmed? He's been speaking to you—what has He been saying? Write it down! You'll need what He has spoken for times of discouragement. If He hasn't confirmed your calling, go to Him and ask Him to. If He doesn't, question as to whether or not He is truly calling. When God calls, that is your confidence—not yourself, or even the fact of your giftedness—but that He has called and that He will enable.

Final pointers on the study, writing, and speaking aspect of the ministry:

- Don't compare yourself to other teachers/speakers. You can *learn* from others but don't compare yourself to them. You'll freeze! It will make you ineffective.
- Determine to deliver well-prepared messages.
- Start early—don't make the mistake of last-minute preparation.
- Don't strive—trust the Holy Spirit—but don't be lax.
- Don't look so hard that you can't see!
- Study and then let there be time for absorption and the voice of the Holy Spirit.
- Let God show you what and how He wants you to teach. You are different than any other teacher. The group you're teaching is different than any other group. *Do it the way He shows you!*

CHAPTER 10
Be Valiant

"For our struggle is not against flesh and blood, but against the rulers, against the powers, against the world forces of this darkness, against the spiritual forces of wickedness in the heavenly places."
Ephesians 6:12

We'll be looking at the subject of conflict in this chapter, and we'll be looking at it through the story of Nehemiah, the wall-builder. Now why would anyone care if you were building a wall? They wouldn't, unless of course the wall you were building was for the Lord and, in particular, for His beloved Jerusalem. In the story of Nehemiah, that is exactly the case. You see, conflict begins when we begin to serve the Lord, and our conflict isn't against flesh and blood, but against the rulers of darkness—spiritual forces that are determined to keep people like you and me and Nehemiah from accomplishing the work of the Lord.

Let's look at the story ...

In Chapter 1, Nehemiah heard the news about the walls of Jerusalem being torn down, the gates being burned, and he heard that things were not going well for the people who had returned to Jerusalem. He realized that they were not only in great trouble, but that they were in disgrace as well. So he mourned, and he fasted, and he prayed over the condition of his beloved city.

In Chapter 2, Nehemiah got permission from the king to go and rebuild the city. He began by inspecting the walls and then he made his report to the leaders of Jerusalem, saying, "Let us rebuild the wall of Jerusalem and rid ourselves of this disgrace!" (Nehemiah 2:17 NLT). To which they responded, "Good! Let's rebuild the wall!" They were in! And Scripture then makes the great and important announcement, "So they began the good work" (Nehemiah 2:18 NLT).

Now, the first mention that something is amiss comes up in Nehemiah 2:10, where the enemies of the work are first mentioned. This is what it says, "But when Sanballat the Horonite and Tobiah the Ammonite official heard of my arrival, they were very angry that someone had come who was interested in helping Israel."

And verse 19 goes on to say, "But when Sanballat, Tobiah, and Geshem the Arab heard of our plan, they scoffed contemptuously [in other words, with contempt]. 'What are you doing, rebelling against the king like this?'"

But Nehemiah took a firm stand against them from the get go and he said, "The God of heaven will help us succeed. We his servants will start rebuilding this wall. But you have no stake or claim in Jerusalem" (verse 20 NLT).

Those are interesting words. They had no stake or claim in the work that was going on in Jerusalem. And we need to remember that about our spiritual enemies. They have no stake or claim on the work we do for the kingdom.

And so the work begins, and before very long, surprise, surprise, the attack begins. Nehemiah 4:1-3 NLT says,

> "Sanballat was very angry when he learned that we were rebuilding the wall. He flew into a rage and mocked the Jews, saying in front of his friends and the Samarian army officers, 'What does this bunch of poor, feeble Jews think they are doing? Do they think they can build the wall in a day if they offer enough sacrifices? Look at those charred stones they are pulling out of the rubbish and using again!' Tobiah the

Ammonite, who was standing beside him, remarked, 'That stone wall would collapse if even a fox walked along the top of it.'"

In response, Nehemiah prayed: "Hear us, O our God, for we are being mocked. May their scoffing fall back on their own heads, and may they themselves become captives in a foreign land! Do not ignore their guilt. Do not blot out their sins, for they have provoked you to anger here in the presence of the builders" (verses 4-5 NLT).

Wow—that was quite a prayer! Do not ignore their guilt? Do not blot out their sins? Why would Nehemiah pray this way? Because Nehemiah recognized what this was—that it wasn't something small, in fact it was something huge—they were mocking the work of God, which is sacred.

And Nehemiah 4:6 gives us the encouraging report: "At last the wall was completed to half its original height around the entire city, for the people had worked very hard" (NLT). I love the way the NKJV says it, it says, "for the people had a mind to work." Isn't that great?

So the presence of an enemy did not deter the work, the mocking and derision of the enemy did not deter the work, and, in fact, the work was progressing very nicely!

So we read in Nehemiah 4:7, "But when Sanballat and Tobiah and the Arabs, Ammonites, and Ashdodites heard that the work was going ahead and the gaps in the wall were being repaired, they became furious" (NLT).

Now I want to stop and look at that verse for a minute, because something interesting has happened. In Nehemiah 2:10 we were introduced to Sanballat the Horonite and Tobiah the Ammonite. In verse 19 of that chapter there was another name added—Geshem the Arab. But here in Nehemiah 4:7 we have a whole list of enemies—Sanballat, and Tobiah, and the Arabs, and the Ammonites, and the Ashdodites!

Now, look at Nehemiah 4:8: "They *all* made plans to come and fight against Jerusalem" (NLT, emphasis added). This was not a little matter! At first the enemies were just individual men—Sanballat, Tobiah, and Geshem. Now we see they are *armies* of men. Men who were probably not even *comrades* before this occasion now had a common hatred—the Jews, and a common purpose—to stop the rebuilding of the wall, which promised the people of Jerusalem protection and strength as a nation.

We can also note that these warring factors were coming from all directions—Sanballat and the Samaritans from the north, Tobiah and the Ammonites from the east, the Arabs from the south, and the Ashdodites from the west.

Have you ever felt like that's what was happening to you—evil coming against you from every direction? That's how it was for Nehemiah and for Jerusalem.

The NLT says it this way: "They all made plans to come and fight against Jerusalem and to bring about confusion there."

The NIV says it this way: "They all plotted together to come and fight against Jerusalem and stir up trouble against it."

The very obvious subject of the verses we are looking at in Nehemiah 4 is spiritual warfare. Enemies of God coming against the work of God. Now, I have to admit, when I come to a passage like this and see that the subject is spiritual warfare, my very first impression is, ugh!!! I don't even want to go there. There are so many other good things to talk about. And besides, I've had enough spiritual warfare in my years of ministry to last me a lifetime!

You see, it has not been that long since I was engaged in what was the most difficult battle in my walk with the Lord. I have just felt in the last few years that I may have come through it—so it's not a subject that I am naturally drawn to. But I realize that is probably the very reason He wants me to share on this subject with you—maybe not even so much for you, but for me!

- Satan didn't want Nehemiah to complete the work God gave him to do.

- Satan doesn't want me to complete the work God gives me to do.

- Satan won't want you to complete the work God gives you to do.

If you are called into ministry—you will find yourself engaged in battle. It's that simple. There is no way around it!

And look at how the warfare escalates—

- In Nehemiah 2:10—the NASB says, they were *displeased.*

- In Nehemiah 2:19—we saw that they held the work in *contempt* (that means as low, worthless, despised).

- In Nehemiah 4:1—we saw that they were *furious* and *mocked* the work and the workers.

- In Nehemiah 4:8—they have *all* plotted together to fight against Jerusalem.

And you know what? I hate to tell you this, but that is how it will be for us, as well. At first the enemy will come against us in smaller ways (although it always seems big!). If we continue on with the work, the attacks will escalate. If we still continue on, the enemy will get furious and do whatever it takes to stop the work and to stop us.

I know this may sound a little melodramatic, but I really feel that there was a time in my ministry that the enemy was trying to get me to quit. And I will also tell you that there were moments when I thought that sounded like it might be a good idea! But I know the Lord has kept me.

I have a friend who, over a period of several years, continued to give me 2 Chronicles 15:7: "But you, be strong and do not lose courage, for there is reward for your work." The NIV uses the words "do not give up."

I can't tell you how thankful I am today for that friend and for that word.

- ✛ Are you being troubled by the enemy today? Don't give up.
- ✛ Are you being battered and tormented? Don't give up.
- ✛ Are you becoming weary in well-doing? Don't give up.

Because if you do, you'll be playing right into the hand of the enemy—and that's the last thing you want to do!

Let's look at what Nehemiah did, because I love it! Nehemiah 4:9 begins with three simple words, "But we prayed ..." The enemies were furious, they were coming at him from every side, and his response is simply, *but we prayed*.

Considering the desperate circumstances, does this help you to understand the importance and power of prayer? It was the first line of offense against the armies of the enemy. "But we prayed to our God and guarded the city day and night to protect ourselves" (verse 9 NLT).

Do you remember what happened on September 11, 2001? Of course you do! Evil terrorists came into our country to destroy our people, to destroy our strongholds—the twin towers and the pentagon (extremely significant places in our country), to destroy our peace, and to destroy our sense of national security.

What did we do as a result of 9/11? The first thing we did was to determine who the enemy was. And then we set up a series of offensive and defensive maneuvers.

Offensively, we began to work on locating the enemies of our country. We infiltrated their territory, ultimately going to war against them. Defensively, we set up a guard over our country (if you've been to an airport since 9/11, you know what I'm talking about), to protect ourselves from more attacks in the future.

That is exactly what Nehemiah did! His offensive weapon was prayer—through prayer he went to war against his enemies! His defensive weapon was to set up a guard over the city day and night.

And what are you and I to do when we find ourselves under attack? We're to do the very same thing.

First we determine who the enemy is. Is this thing that's going on in my life just a series of bad circumstances, or is it a calculated strike against me by the enemy of my soul? If I determine it is a strike against me, then I need to strike back immediately in both an offensive and defensive campaign. In other words, I need to pray to my God and set up a guard over the city of my heart and mind.

Now, I say this as if it is a simple thing to determine and to do. Unfortunately, one of the enemy's greatest weapons against us is confusion. So we are often confused as to what exactly is going on. And so maybe my prayers in the early stages of warfare are not nearly as defined and direct as those of Nehemiah.

He knew exactly who the enemies were and he prayed very effectively against them. Maybe I'm not sure exactly what's going on. Maybe I think the enemy is attacking me, but I'm not sure how to express a clear prayer. What am I to do? Still pray.

- ✣ Pray to the Lord about what I am *feeling*.

- ✣ Tell Him all about *what's happening to me*.

- ✣ Tell Him what I *think it might be*.

- ✣ Share with Him what it is that I want *Him to do for me*.

- ✣ And then trust Him to answer that prayer according to what He knows to be the true need and, of course, according to His will.

Listen to what I think may be the best verses we have on prayer. Romans 8:26-27 NLT says, "And the Holy Spirit helps us in our distress. For we don't even know what we should pray for, nor how we should pray. But the Holy Spirit prays for us with groanings that cannot be expressed in words. And the Father who knows all hearts knows what the Spirit is saying, for the Spirit pleads for us believers in harmony with God's own will."

Isn't that a hopeful passage on prayer? I am so blessed to know that prayer is powerful and that it is also spiritual. It is not according to the law, but according to grace. We don't need to be afraid of prayer. We don't need to be afraid of *ourselves* in prayer. We just need to pray.

Do you ever feel like you haven't prayed enough or maybe you didn't pray the right words or maybe you left out something that was vitally important? That's the enemy! He wants to keep you confused and he wants to keep you doubting—he wants to keep you trusting in *yourself* and what *you're doing* and if *you're getting everything right*. And what a trap that is! God just wants you to believe. And He wants you to trust in Him.

And how do you and I go about setting up a guard, night and day? We simply begin to think defensively.

Listen to 1 Peter 5:8-9 AMPLIFIED, "Be well balanced (temperate, sober of mind), be vigilant and cautious at all times; for that enemy of yours, the devil, roams around like a lion roaring [in fierce hunger], seeking someone to seize upon and devour. Withstand him; be firm in faith [against his onset—rooted, established, strong, immovable, and determined], knowing that the same (identical) sufferings are appointed to your brotherhood (the whole body of Christians) throughout the world."

Now, there's so much to be said about spiritual warfare—and we could get into a real in-depth study on this subject—but I love the simple thing that we read right off the bat in that verse. It begins with, "Be well balanced (temperate, sober of mind), vigilant and cautious at all times ..."

Isn't that simple? Sometimes we want all the big weapons and here we are given such a simple one—be well-balanced. What does that mean in the way of defense? It means be well-balanced! That's a defense in itself!

Living a well-balanced life immediately takes power away from the devil. He's looking for someone to devour—don't make it easy for him! When you are doing the normal things in life in a moderate and well-balanced way, you take a lot of opportunities away from him. If you're living out on the edge—then he has all kinds of ways he can pull the rug out from under you—and he will!

So live a well-balanced, temperate, and sober life. Be vigilant and cautious at all times. That means be on the look out! You already know that he's there and that he is just looking for an opportunity to pounce on you—be watching for him. Expect the attack. Then you will be more able to thwart it.

If you're in ministry, then you already know he's coming to get you. It's the night before a meeting that you are supposed to speak at. Eat properly. Have your preparations for the day of ministry in order. Have your clothes ready. Be balanced and sober about the situation! Get to bed on time. Don't drink caffeine before bed (that's for me!).

That's the first line of defense.

But now, you've done all that and still there you are lying in bed wide awake at 3:00 in the morning and you suddenly remember that awful thing you did when you were 18. Guilt overwhelms you. How could God possibly use me? What was I thinking when I said yes? Guess who???

Or your husband comes home from work the night before a big event and he's in a bad mood—and before you know it you're in one too! Or the car breaks down on the way to the church. Or the kids get sick. Or you get a kitchen full of ants. For me, it's usually migraines. And, although it may take you a little while to realize that this hindrance is from the enemy—because you are in defensive mode, eventually you do.

And when you do, you immediately go into the offensive mode and you begin to pray! And, if you're smart, you'll get other people praying for you!

Let's look for a minute at Ephesians 6, which is the definitive passage on spiritual warfare. It teaches us who our enemies are and what we are to do to be able to stand against them.

Verses 10-13 say, "Finally, be strong in the Lord, and in the strength of His might. Put on the full armor of God, that you may be able to stand firm against the schemes of the devil. For our struggle is not against flesh and blood, but against the rulers, against the powers, against the world forces of this darkness, against the spiritual forces of wickedness in the heavenly places. Therefore, take up the full armor of God, that you may be able to resist in the evil day, and having done everything, to stand firm."

Let's take stock here:

- In whom are we to be strong?
- Whose strength are we to lean on?
- Whose armor are we to wear? (Putting on the armor is clothing yourself with Christ!)
- And what are we ultimately to do?

Verse 13 ends with the same two words that verse 14 begins with: stand firm! That's what Nehemiah did. And that's what I have had to do. And that's what you will have to do, too.

I remember at one of my lowest points in the years of my greatest battle, I was teaching on a Friday night at a women's retreat, encouraging the ladies to believe and trust God, and the whole time (I mean right then and there as I was delivering the message) I was in an all out war with the enemy.

God was so faithful to enable me to deliver the message that first night, but as soon as I was done, the enemy was there oppressing me in my spirit. I remember going to my room that night feeling so defeated—and yet knowing that the next morning I needed to get up and speak again.

I felt very alone and vulnerable, and then the Lord ministered to me. He spoke one word to me—it was *endure*. And I knew two things with that word—I knew the battle wasn't over, but I knew that it would be! And I realized, again, who was in control—God was. And He had given me the word—I was to endure. With that word came peace and I remember that night I went to sleep in victory.

We are promised victory. So don't let the enemy make you think you will surely be defeated. No, in fact, you will surely be the victor! That's what Ephesians 6 is really about—putting our complete trust in God, for what He has already done for us and what He is willing and able to do for us today and in the future.

Psalm 60:12 says, "Through God we shall do valiantly, and it is He who will tread down our adversaries."

1 Corinthians 15:57 NIV says, "But thanks be to God! He gives us the victory through our Lord Jesus Christ."

Romans 8:37 says, "But in all these things we overwhelmingly conquer through Him who loved us."

Amy Carmichael says it this way: "Let us take victory, not defeat, for granted."[1]

And 2 Chronicles 20:15 NIV says, "This is what the Lord says to you: 'Do not be afraid or discouraged because of this vast army. For the battle is not yours, but God's."

So don't be afraid and don't think that you have to count entirely on yourself in this battle. It would scare me to death if I thought that were true! Trust God to show you what you need to see and to tell you what you need to know. Trust Him that if you need to see something you haven't yet seen or if you need to know something you don't yet know—He will make sure to get that information to you. And then do your best.

In 1 Corinthians 15:58, after Paul tells of the ultimate victory that we have in Christ, over the ultimate enemy, death, he finishes with these words:

NASB—Therefore, my beloved brethren, be steadfast, immoveable, always abounding in the work of the Lord, knowing that your toil is not in vain in the Lord."

NCV—"So my dear brothers and sisters, stand strong. Do not let anything change you. Always give yourselves fully to the work of the Lord, because you know that your work in the Lord is never wasted."

The Message—"With all this going for us, my dear, dear friends, stand your ground. And don't hold back. Throw yourselves into the work of the Master, confident that nothing you do for him is a waste of time or effort."

Amen!!!

CHAPTER 11
Count the Cost

"From now on let no one cause trouble for me, for I bear on my
body the brandmarks of Jesus."
Galatians 6:17

There is a cost to effective leadership. And I dare say some of you, if not all of you, already know that quite well! This is a subject that, for whatever reason, has always been sort of fascinating to me. Certainly not because I like trials; maybe because I like to encourage. And this is an area in which we greatly need encouragement, because it is the thing that can ultimately make or break a leader.

We often say that we're willing to pay the price. We say it in many ways:

✜ "Oh Lord, I'll do anything for You."

✜ "I'll go through anything You want to take me through."

✜ "I'll never leave you; I'll always love you."

And I know we truly mean those words when we say them and, thankfully, the Lord looks at our heart and the motivation of the words we say.

But—I think we often make those declarations with what I call a romantic notion. Romantically thinking that when we say we'll go through anything for Him, it will somehow be a lovely and wonderful thing when we do.

The truth of the matter is that the trials we may be called to go through will probably be anything but lovely and wonderful. They will be real. They will be hard. They will hurt deeply. They may be ugly, and dark, and there may even be sin involved.

We say, in our innocence, "Anything Lord," and then He takes one little thing away and we think we're going to die.

And then, there's the sin nature in us. Maybe He will allow it to rise to the surface. Ouch!

Think of Peter. He actually denied the Lord—the one He loved so much that just hours before He had pledged that even if all the others left him, he, Peter, would not. It was one of those romantic pledges, don't you think?

"Oh yes Lord—I will go anywhere with you—even to death." Oh really? When the rubber met the road, things were a bit different. You see, Peter had to see what was really in him. Do you think that was pretty?

The trials the Lord allows us to go through in order for us to really be useful are not usually very pretty. I wonder, are we prepared for that?

The Cost. That is the subject. And remember, we're talking here about the call to leadership—real spiritual leadership. Not necessarily about holding a particular position at church. Certainly that can be true spiritual leadership, but it isn't necessarily. We're talking about that true leadership that is conferred by God alone and is authoritative because it is empowered by His Spirit.

I love many things the book *Spiritual Leadership* has to say about the cost.

- ✣ It tells us that the cost is bought on the time payment plan—a further installment each new day, and when payment ceases, leadership wanes. Interesting.

- ✣ It tells us that the degree that we allow the cross of Christ to work in us will be the measure in which the resurrection life of Christ can be manifested through us. Wow!

- ✣ It tells us that to evade the cross is to forfeit leadership.

And I love the words the chapter on the cost starts with. It says this:

"No one need to aspire to leadership in the work of God who is not prepared to pay a price greater than his contemporaries and colleagues are willing to pay. True leadership always exacts a heavy toll on the whole man and the more effective the leadership, the higher the price to be paid."

So the question to us is—are we willing to pay the price that is required for effective spiritual leadership?

A thought we need to tuck away in the backs of our minds as we consider this subject is that God uses broken people.

- ✣ Think again of Peter—the denier.
- ✣ Of Paul—the persecutor.
- ✣ Of Timothy—the timid.
- ✣ Of John Mark—the deserter.

Peter's pride had to be broken. Paul was zealous—but not according to truth. He had to redirect his passion in accordance with truth. Timothy would have to be made strong. John Mark would have to learn discipline.

And all of them—and all of us—will be called on to share in the sufferings of Christ. That's all part of the cost.

I had an opportunity to share at a women's retreat several years ago on the subject of faith and commitment.

The title of the retreat was, *"Women of Faith, Committed to the Call."* When I considered what it was that the Lord would have me to share on that particular subject, I came to the conclusion that He wanted me to share my own experience of what it was to be a *woman of faith to be committed to the call.*

And my message really came down to three things—the call, the cost, and the commitment.

Now I have already shared the call with you. I shared how the Lord called me into ministry quite apart from myself. I had nothing in me, as far as I knew, to fulfill the ministry He called me to, but it seems that He had been preparing me all along for that very call, unbeknownst to myself.

I told you that I was just like you, a very ordinary person. And that, although I didn't know a soul at my church, God knew me, and by a very interesting chain of events, called me into ministry.

What I haven't shared with you yet was what took place after I was called. And that's really where the cost and the commitment come in.

My first few years of ministry were some of the most difficult times my husband and I ever experienced. We had three years that started right about the time I began to teach of almost constant and diverse trials. And it was really about then that I began to realize, probably for the first time, that there was a cost to service.

There was a brief retrieve for a few years, and then another wave. This new wave of trials lasted longer and was far more intense. I remember somewhere in the middle of this trial the Lord ministered two verses to me:

John 11:4—"This sickness is not unto death, but for the glory of God, that the Son of God may be glorified by it."

John 12:24—"Unless a grain of wheat falls into the earth and dies, it remains by itself alone; but if it dies it bears much fruit."

On the day He gave me those two verses I remember knowing that something very hard was coming—something that would look or feel like death, but wouldn't be, and that in the end, God would be glorified.

The last year of that trial (which lasted eight years) was 1996. And in that year it truly seemed as if we weren't going to make it. And you know how it is when you are in a trial—you are where you are and there is nothing that you can do to change the situation, try as you may.

I remember coming to the conclusion during the hardest days of this seemingly unending trial that, although the Lord was surely teaching my husband and me some valuable lessons, there was an element of the trial that I began to realize came simply because of my ministry of teaching God's Word. God was doing a deeper work. There is a cost that comes with the call.

Listen to the wisdom in a chapter in *Spiritual Leadership*:

> "It is noteworthy that only once did Jesus say that He was leaving His disciples an example, and that was when He washed their feet—an example of servanthood. And only once did any other writer say that He had left an example—and that was an example of suffering (1 Peter 2:21—"For you have been called for this purpose, since Christ also suffered for you, leaving you an example for you to follow in His steps"). Thus the thought of suffering and servanthood are linked, even as they were in the life of the Lord. And is the servant greater than his Lord?" No!

Somehow we made it through the great trial of 96! And we had another few years of relative quiet. Then, in March 2000, things began to turn again. There were a series of things that started small, but escalated very quickly.

At our women's retreat that year, there was a small incident that sort of deflated my ego. Nothing huge, but significant enough for me to say to the Lord, "Thank You for being willing to trust me with that."

I was pondering what had happened, feeling a little low, and some other things were on my mind, and at some point during the evening session the Lord spoke to me. Somewhere in the midst of what was being shared that night the Lord revealed to me an area of sin in my heart—it was an exact and specific word—*pride*.

It was quite a revelation. I truly hadn't seen it. But when the word came I knew it was the Lord and I knew it was true, and I also knew something else instinctively, and that was that I couldn't fix this problem. The Lord would have to do this.

I went home from that retreat realizing that the Lord had some deep work to do in my heart and asking Him—even begging Him—to do it.

A few weeks later I had to share at a big women's function. I was actually helping someone else, and because I was helping her, I was sharing more from what was on her heart than what was on mine. I felt uncomfortable with the message and was not happy with the way I delivered it. (And that's certainly not the first time or the last time that has happened!)

But the theme Scripture of that conference was, "Not by might, nor by strength, but by my Spirit, saith the Lord" (Zechariah 4:6). And I remember that day feeling as if the Lord was saying to me, "You know what Linda? It doesn't really matter what you think or feel about your message." And a word came through loud and clear to me that day— "It's not about you, it's about Me!"

A couple of weeks later, I was reading *My Utmost for His Highest* one morning. Romans 6:6 was the verse—"Knowing this that our old self was crucified with Him that our body of sin might be done away with, that we should no longer be slaves of sin."

Oswald Chambers said, "Am I prepared to let the Spirit of God search me until I know what the disposition of sin is—the thing that lusts against the Spirit of God in me? Then if so, will I agree with God's verdict on that disposition of sin—that it should identified with the death of Jesus? I cannot reckon myself dead unto sin unless I have been through this radical issue of will before God." And other statement— "Haul yourself up take a time alone with God, make the moral decision and say—Lord identify me with thy death until I know that sin is dead in me."

Well—that devotion really ministered to me. The next morning when I got up, I found myself turning back to that day again. It seemed to be speaking to me and so I spent time meditating on the thoughts there and I decided to pray that very prayer.

He had already shown me what the disposition of my sin was—pride—now I prayed the prayer, "Lord identify me with Your death until I know that sin is dead in me."

Have you ever prayed a prayer like that and had the distinct feeling that the Lord was going to take you up on it?

We always want the Lord to do the thing we're asking for when we pray, but there have been a couple of times when I literally felt right then and there that He would take me up on my prayer, and that there would be a high price to be paid for the answer.

This was one of those times. And He did. And there was—beginning that day.

That day, I believe, the first death blow was struck. And I was sent reeling. I didn't know what to do—there must be something I should do! I obviously had done something very wrong. Obviously my spiritual warfare wasn't up to par. Somehow I needed to fix something! But I had no idea what or how!

Well the Lord ministered to me through Oswald Chambers (again!) a simple word that gave me some comfort and direction as I wondered what it was that I either should have done, or should do now. This was the word:

> "The weakest saint can experience the power of the Deity of the Son of God if once he is willing to 'let go.' Any strand of our own energy will blur the life of Jesus. We have to keep letting go, and slowly and surely the great full life of God will invade us in every part, and men will take knowledge of us that we have been with Jesus."

I decided that night (the night of the morning I prayed for death; the night of the day the death blow came), to let go and simply move forward with all that I already knew. What I really knew was that God was answering my prayer and I needed to let Him work.

A couple of weeks went by and it was my turn to teach at the Bible study. I was truly that weakest saint at this point, still very much feeling the effects of that blow. But, I was scheduled to speak, and so I did. That morning, after giving a difficult message, a friend of mine came up to me with a small piece of paper in her shaking hands. She said, "The Lord wants me to give this to you." I didn't even want to take it, but of course I knew I had to. As I opened it there were the words: "Peter, Peter (Linda, Linda), Satan has demanded to sift you like wheat, but I have prayed for you, that your faith may not fail."

My friend quietly said, "Linda, the Lord is praying for you." But I couldn't hear that, all I could see were the words that said that Satan had demanded to sift me like wheat, and I knew it was already taking place.

I was getting ready to speak at a retreat right at that time, and I was in such a hard place personally—but the Lord ministered to me.

I just want to share a couple of the things He ministered to me—because I know that there are some who are reading this that may be in an equally difficult place and might need an encouraging word. Notice the common denominator as you read these quotes.

Three days in a row *Streams in the Desert* met me exactly where I was, with exactly what I needed:

✤ Day 1—
   "He will do this" (Psalm 37:5).
"I once believed that after I prayed, it was my responsibility to do everything in my power to bring about the answer. Yet God taught me a better way and showed me that self-effort always hinders His work. He also revealed that when I prayed and had confident trust in Him for something, He simply wanted me to wait in an attitude of praise and do only what He told me. Sitting still and doing nothing

except trusting in the Lord causes a feeling of uncertainty, and there is often a tremendous temptation to take the battle into our own hands. We all know how difficult it is to rescue a drowning person, who tries to help his rescuer, and it is equally difficult for the Lord to fight our battles for us when we insist upon trying to fight them ourselves."

"Spiritual forces cannot work while we are trusting earthly forces."

✟ Day 2—
"Stand firm and you will see the deliverance the Lord will bring you today" (Exodus 14:13).

"If for a season He calls me to stand firm, I will acknowledge it as a time for me to renew my strength for greater strides in the future. Impatience will come crying, get up and do something. To stand firm is to wait in sheer idleness. Why is it I think I must be doing something right now, instead of looking to the Lord? He will not only do something—He will do everything!"

✟ Day 3—
"Not by might, nor by power but by my Spirit, saith the Lord" (Zechariah 4:6). (The Scripture God had ministered to me at the women's conference.) I felt clearly that the word the Lord was speaking to me was, "Let Go, Linda and let Me do it."

The next year of Bible study came and went: another difficult year. I remember thinking that the enemy was in my face the entire year. It was a constant battle.

The difference between the battle I was now facing was that it was personal. Most of my difficult trials before had been circumstantial. This was personal—kind of like a direct assault.

It was during that year that my dear friend Christi gave me the verse: "But as for you, be strong and do not give up, for your work will be rewarded" (2 Chronicles 15:7).

By the end of that year of Bible study, I was weary. The Lord ministered to me as He gave me my confirmation Scripture for returning the next year—"Therefore, since through God's mercy we have this ministry, we do not lose heart" (2 Corinthians 4:1).

So, I continued walking forward. The next year came and went—but the most difficult time was coming. The year was 2002, and I would label this year in my life, "loss." I lost something very dear to my heart that year, and that loss made the things that were happening in ministry all the harder.

And at the end of the Bible study year in 2002 there was yet another blow, again, very personal. And there was one particular day that I was simply broken. It was one of those days that I didn't know how I would ever be able to go forward. I was crushed. I was in my car after a difficult meeting and there was a message on the radio. I came into it in the middle, so I didn't even know who was speaking. I found out later that it was Priscilla Evens. And you know what? She was speaking just to me!

I pulled out a paper as I was driving down the street (not a wise thing to do), and I scribbled a few of the things she said—this is how I wrote it (I'm not certain this is how she said it, but this is how I wrote it!):

> "He wants me to learn how to walk with my head held high in the midst of my trial. Not to be delivered from it ... knowing who I am regardless of the circumstances. God will be faithful to me. When we are faithful, He is faithful. Even when I feel I've been cleaned out, for His name's sake, I will press on."

And you know what? That's the commitment! Even when I feel I've been cleaned out, for His name's sake, I will press on.

Priscilla told a wonderful story that day on the radio—something I have shared many times over. She told the story of a woman who was on a journey, and on that journey she came to a huge body of water. There didn't appear to be any way she could ever cross the water—she would drown! But that was the only way to continue on her journey.

So, she turned to the right and walked for a long distance, but there was no end to the water. So she turned to the left and walked on and on, but still no end. She finally came to the realization that the only way to continue on her journey was to cross the uncrossable body of water. So she put one foot in the water, and it was about two inches deep. She put her other foot in the water, and it was still only two inches deep. She continued putting one foot in front of the other, and believe it or not, the entire body of water was only two inches deep!

That was the most wonderful picture for me that day. I felt like the Lord was saying, "Just take one step at a time Linda, you won't go under, every step in itself will be do-able, only two inches deep."

Now, the interesting thing was that she didn't actually interpret the story in the same way that I was interpreting it as I listened! She turned the story around at the end and she said:

"Have you ever met a Christian who just looked so together? She looks the part, she speaks the part, the minute you meet her you think you're in the presence of a super saint, but then you get to know her and you find out that all that you thought you saw in her was really only two inches deep?"

Her application had to do with the sad potential of you or me being a two-inch-deep Christian: looking good on the outside, but having no depth.

That interpretation spoke to me as clearly as the one I thought she was making. I don't want to be a two-inch-deep Christian. And I know you don't either. I knew the Lord was saying, "Let me make you more."

The Word that hung over my heart those years was, "He must increase, I must decrease" (John 3).

In a book called *Rediscovering Holiness*, J I Packer has written a wonderful chapter called *Growing Downward*. Listen to what he says:

"We grow up into Christ by growing down into lowliness. Off-loading our fantasies of omnicompetence, we start trying to be trustful, obedient, dependent, patient and willing in our relationship to God. We give up our dreams of being greatly admired for doing wonderfully well. We begin teaching ourselves unemotionally and matter of factly to recognize that we are not likely ever to appear, or actually to be, much of a success by the world's standards. We bow to events that rub our noses in the reality of our own weaknesses, and we look to God for strength quietly to cope. It is impossible at the same time to give the impression both that I am a great Christian and that Jesus Christ is a great Master. So the Christian will practice curling up small as it were, so that in and through him or her, the Savior may show himself great. That is what I mean by growing downward."

In the chapter entitled, "The Cost of Leadership," in his book *Spiritual Leadership*, J Oswald Sanders says this:

"Dr. Samuel M. Zwemer recalls the striking fact that the only thing Jesus took pains to show after His resurrection was His scars. His disciples recognized neither Him nor His message on the Emmaus road. Not until He broke the bread and they possibly saw the scars were their sensibilities aroused.

"When He stood in the midst of His demoralized disciples in the upper room after the resurrection, He showed them both His hands and feet. Scars are the authentic marks of faithful discipleship and true spiritual leadership. Nothing moves people more than the print of the nails and the marks of the spear. Those are test of sincerity that no one can challenge, as Paul well knew. 'From now on let now one cause trouble for me, for I bear on my body the brandmarks of Jesus'" (Galatians 6:17).

Amy Carmichael has written a poem that I think says it best:

> Hast thou no scar?
> No hidden scar on foot, or side, or hand?
> I hear thee sung as mighty in the land.
> I hear them hail thy bright ascendant star:
> Hast thou no scar?

Hast thou no wound?
Yet, I was wounded by the archers, spent.
Leaned me against the tree to die, and rent.
By ravening beasts that compassed me, I swooned:
Hast thou no wound?

No wound? No scar?
Yes, as the master shall the servant be.
And pierced are the feet that follow Me;
But thine are whole. Can he have followed far
Who has no wound? No Scar?

I have a theory about scars. I was thinking one day about the way men who have been in the war might show each other their battle scars as a sort of prized possession. "I got this one in the big war." "That's nothing, look at this one!" And so on and so forth.

I was thinking on that particular day that I would actually be ashamed to stand before Jesus without any scars. Remember, scars are the authentic marks of faithful discipleship and true spiritual leadership.

There is a cost to serving Christ, but I sometimes wonder if, in the end, we'll find out that the cost will actually be the reward.

APPENDIX A
My Favorite Books!

"When you come bring the cloak which I left at Troas with Carpus, and the books, especially the parchments."
2 Timothy 4:13

Books—what could be more wonderful? When I am asked on a questionnaire what kinds of activities I enjoy, I know they probably mean something physical, but I always answer the same way—I love to read. And I'm very thankful that I have passed that love on to at least one of my children—my son is also an avid reader!

Spurgeon has said this about reading: "Master those books you have. Read them thoroughly. Bathe in them until they saturate you ... In reading let your motto be 'much, not many.'"[1]

I loved reading that, because that truly is my philosophy in reading. Although I consider myself an avid reader, I have gained great things from a small number of books which I have gone back to over and over again throughout the years. I am sharing my favorites with you! Perhaps you will gain from them as I have.

Devotions
My Utmost for His Highest
by Oswald Chambers
I've been reading this devotional for over 35 years! If you are reading it for the first time, give it some time—it's a little difficult to get into—but once you do, you may end up saying, as I have, that Oswald Chambers has become your spiritual mentor.

Streams in the Desert
by Mrs. Charles E. Cowman
I only began reading this devotional about fifteen years ago and now I hate to miss it, even for a day! It is a deeply refreshing touch of perspective on the love, comfort, and hope that is found in the Lord, especially in the midst of difficulty. Next to the Bible, it positively carried me through my last dark trial.

Leadership
Spiritual Leadership
by J. O. Sanders
The best book on spiritual leadership I've ever read!

A Tale of Three Kings
by Gene Edwards
A book that teaches submission to authority through the struggles of David with Saul and later with Absalom. A must read for anyone in Christian ministry.

Biographies
Biographies are my all-time favorite books. I have read many—I am sharing those that have inspired me the most deeply.

Amy Carmichael of Dohnavur
by Frank L. Houghton
Just the introduction to this book brings me to my knees.

George Mueller, Delighted in God!
by Roger Steer
Be inspired by a man who had great faith in a great and faithful God.

Hudson Taylor's Spiritual Secret
by Dr. and Mrs. Howard Taylor
Another great story of personal faith and the faithfulness of God.

Rees Howells Intercessor
by Norman Grubb
This book grabbed me like no other biography I have yet read. It is powerful!

Seven Guides to Effective Prayer
by Colin Whittaker
Deeply inspiring biographies of seven great prayer warriors.

They Found the Secret
by V. Raymond Edman
Twenty-six short biographies pointing to the defining moment when each one learned to live "on Christ" by the power of His Holy Spirit.

Various Spiritual Subjects

The Pursuit of God
by A.W. Tozer
Maybe the first deep touch of a spiritual book on my life.

Let Go
by Fénelon
Sit at the feet of one of the great saints and catch from him something of his intimate relationship with God. God led me to this book many years ago when I desperately needed to learn to "let go."

The Green Letters
by Miles J. Stanford
This book helped me understand how sin, failure, and need (each of which I have known in abundance!) lead to growth in faith—the theme being "Not I, but Christ."

Hinds Feet on High Places
by Hannah Hurnard

Although there are so many books that have ministered to me deeply—this simple little allegory about a young girl named Much Afraid has met me in places of difficulty and given me the hope and courage that I not only <u>could</u> go on, but that I can live in the High Places right here during this lifetime!

"An old writer who adopted the pseudonym Cladius Clear suggested that a booklover could divide his books as he would people. A few he would term 'lovers,' and they would be the books he would take with him if he were exiled. Others, and more than in the first class, he would call 'friends.' The majority he would designate 'acquaintances,' books with which he was on nodding terms and to which he occasionally referred."[2]

During a study on the book *Spiritual Leadership*, the question was asked—"What three books would you take if you were being sent into exile?" Now for a booklover, that's a hard one! But I came down to these three: my Bible (of course!), *My Utmost for His Highest,* and *Hinds Feet on High Places.*

Whatever you end you reading, I hope you realize that books are a wonderful gift that we have been given. Enjoy!

APPENDIX B
Study Guide

✣

I was having dinner one evening with a dear friend before attending the final night of her summer study and I told her that I had finished my book and shared with her the list of chapter titles. As she looked them over, she mentioned that she might want to use my book for the study she would do the next summer. I sort of pondered what she said, thinking inside, "I wonder how exactly she would do that?" I asked her what she was thinking and as we talked over how that could be done, we realized that it would be very helpful if there were questions to go along with each chapter of the book. I loved the idea immediately!

Don't we love to share our experiences in ministry? And don't we especially love to share those special moments when we have heard a specific word from the Lord, or had a meaningful experience with the Lord? The following questions will give you that opportunity.

I pray this will be an added benefit for you, and that the Lord will remind you, as you read each chapter of this book, of the *many things* He has done in your life and for you in the years that you have walked with Him. May He richly bless your study!

Procedures for study group:

✢ Have each participant read the chapter of the book you will be discussing and prepare her thoughts on the questions asked.

✢ Begin your group-time with a prayer.

✢ Encourage each woman to share her thoughts. Make it a safe place for sharing both the positive and even the negative feelings she might have. Because these are personal questions with personal answers, there is no right or wrong!

✢ Take time after the sharing-time is over for prayer. This might be a great time to pray for the one who is discouraged, struggling, or even better, to pray with those who are rejoicing!

Chapter 1
Catch the Vision!

1. How are you using your hours and your days? Is there anything could do differently that would open the way for you to give more of yourself to the kingdom of God?

2. Have you ever made the decision to devote your life entirely to accomplish God's will here on earth? If you have, share your thoughts about that decision. If you haven't, do you want to do so now?

3. Has God ever spoken a word to you similar to the word, "I can do great things through you"? Has He ever revealed to you that your life mattered for the kingdom of God? Share your experience.

4. If you could do *anything* your heart desired for the kingdom of God (in other words, if time and expense were no issue), what would it be?

5. What is the most important thing you gleaned from your study of this chapter?

Chapter 2
Listen for the Call

1. What have you been asked to do in ministry that you knew was "sovereignly assigned" by God? How did the Lord "call" you to that good work?

Study Guide

2. What difference does it make to you personally—and to your ministry—to be able to affirm "I am not here by selection of a man or election of a group, but by the sovereign appointment of God"? If you have ever had trouble with submission to authority, how does understanding "the sovereign appointment of God" help your perspective?

3. What is your master passion—or what do you desire it to be? What is your master ambition—or what do you desire it to be (share honestly—so that everyone in the group can be honest!)? What difference will this make in your influence on others?

4. Is there a good work that you are *hoping* God will call you to do? How will you wait? Will you be anxious? Will you be offended if it doesn't come your way?

5. What is the most important thing you gleaned from your study of this chapter?

Chapter 3
Follow the Leader

1. Who is our example in service? How did He serve? In what ways does your service resemble His?

2. What have you learned in this chapter about serving with the right heart and motives? Have you recognized that those you serve are His little flock? How will these thoughts make a difference in the future of your ministry, and what will you do to turn things around in those areas in which you realize you have been lacking?

3. Talk about the gain you have had in ministry. Talk about the loss. What have you learned through each of these things?

4. What difference will it make to the shepherd-leader once she has seen His glory?

5. What is the most important thing you gleaned from your study of this chapter?

Chapter 4
Use Your Gifts/Part 1

1. Share your personal understanding of Ephesians 2:10. (Share what the Lord has spoken to *you* in that verse!)

2. At which stage of ministry do you find yourself at the present time—blooming where you're planted, or using the gifts you've been given? Share some of the things you did when you first stepped out to serve the Lord.

3. Have you ever found yourself neglecting your ministry (and just as importantly, your family) because of the many "good works" you were doing? What do you learn from Acts 6 (specifically verses 1-4)?

4. What have you learned through your own experience about the *good* versus the *best*? Share a story if you have one. What does it mean to you to be using your highest gifts?

5. What is the most important thing you gleaned from your study of this chapter?

Chapter 5
Use Your Gifts/Part 2

1. Share some of things you understand about the gifts of the Spirit.

2. Have you discovered what some of your spiritual gifts are? How did you identify them? Share with the group how you feel "compelled" to use the gifts you have been given.

3. What new appreciation for the spiritual gifts of others have you gotten as you've read this chapter?

4. Have you thought of any new ways in which you could be using the gifts you have been given?

5. What is the most important thing you gleaned from your study of this chapter?

Chapter 6
Be Prepared

1. How would others recognize that you are a person of faith? Share an opportunity you have recently had to display faith in the midst of a difficult situation. What difference did "standing in faith" make to the experience?

2. Share an area in which you have had to learn to discipline yourself. Was it hard? How did you do it? Did it make a difference in any other areas of your life?

3. How important is it to the ministry as a whole that you have a servant's heart? Define what you think that looks like.

4. Name one area that you saw in this chapter that you have a handle on. Name an area that you have realized you need to work on. What will you do?

5. What is the most important thing you gleaned from your study of this chapter?

Chapter 7
Just Say Please

1. Share your thoughts on why it's important for *you* to use good etiquette in ministry. Why is it important to you that *others* use good etiquette while they are performing their ministry?

2. How can you allow the Holy Spirit to have full reign, and yet stay within the time allotted for you to perform your area of ministry?

3. Share what you consider to be your priorities at this time in your life. How can you keep the balance between fulfilling the requirements of your commitment and yet remembering that it is *not* your life—it's only one part of your life?

4. Which of the good etiquette "Bs" do you consider the most important? Which one of them is easiest for you? Which one do you have the most trouble with?

5. What is the most important thing you gleaned from your study of this chapter?

Chapter 8
Take the Lead

1. Come up with your own definition of the words: *lead, leader,* and *leadership*.

2. Explain what you think it means *in your own ministry* for you to *exert yourself to lead*. (In other words, what would it look like for you to take the lead?)

3. Which of the hindrances to effective leadership speaks the most deeply to you? What will you do to be a more effective leader in light of what you have learned here?

4. Consider those three words: *pride*, *perfectionism*, and *performance*. Which is more of a temptation to you? Have you ever felt like you were *performing* in ministry? How can *just being aware of this* make a difference in how you minister?

5. What is the most important thing you gleaned from your study of this chapter?

Chapter 9
Study, Write, Speak!

1. When beginning your study, what are some of the preliminary things you should do before you begin to look at study books like commentaries, etc. See if you can explain what you are attempting to do when you use the inductive method of study.

2. Share your thoughts on the importance of the Holy Spirit in your study and preparation for a message. What message does 1 John 2:27 speak to you?

3. How can you share on a personal level without making your message *all about you*? Why do you think it's important for a speaker/teacher not to share all their troubles and be too specific about their problems?

4. Which of the *practical pointers* on speaking or the *final pointers* on the study/writing/speaking aspect of the ministry helped you the most and why?

5. What is the most important thing you gleaned from your study of this chapter?

Chapter 10
Be Valiant

1. See if you can differentiate the experience of *going through a trial* with the experience of *spiritual warfare*. Share an experience you have had with spiritual warfare in your work for the Lord.

2. Share your understanding of the importance and power of prayer in spiritual warfare. How has prayer been your offensive weapon in your battle with the enemy? How will it be in the future?

3. See if you can explain how being well-balanced can be a defensive weapon against the enemy. Are you well-balanced? Is there anything you might need to do in this area in order to be better protected against those spiritual attacks?

4. Share with the others in your group a few of the words the Lord has spoken to you and a few of the ways He has ministered to you during your distress in the midst of the battle.

5. What is the most important thing you gleaned from your study of this chapter?

Chapter 11
Count the Cost

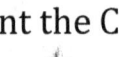

1. Share your experience of what it means to be a *woman of faith, committed to the call.*

2. In what way have you seen personally that there is a cost to effective leadership and that it can't be paid in one lump sum? Do you understand why this might be?

3. How do you think *brokenness* makes a servant of God useful for the work of the ministry?

4. See if you can explain how, when God is taking you through the painful process of "making you a woman of God," self-effort actually hinders His work. When going through the death process, what should you do?

5. What is the most important thing you gleaned from your study of this chapter?

BIBLIOGRAPHY

Chapter 1

[1]Taken from *My Utmost for His Highest* by Oswald Chambers, © 1935 by Dodd Mead & Co., renewed © 1963 by the Chambers Publications Assn., Ltd. Used by permission of Discovery House Publishers, Box 3566, Grand Rapids, MI. All rights reserved. June 7th.

[2]Frank L. Houghton, *Amy Carmichael of Dohnavur*, (Fort Washington, Pennsylvania: Christian Literature Crusade, 1953), p. 49.

[3]J. Oswald Sanders, *Spiritual Leadership,* (Moody Bible Institute of Chicago, 1967, 1980), p. 113.

[4]IBID p. 114.

[5]IBID p. 41.

Chapter 2

[1]J. Oswald Sanders, *Spiritual Leadership*, (Moody Bible Institute of Chicago, 1967, 1980), p. 31.

[2]IBID, p. 20

[3]IBID, p. 20

[4]IBID, p. 19

[5]IBID, p. 20

[6]IBID, p. 24

[7]IBID, p. 31

[8]IBID, p. 20

Chapter 3

[1] J. Vernon McGee, *Thru the Bible with J. Vernon McGee*, (Nashville, Tennessee: Thomas Nelson, Inc., 1983), p. 711.

[2] Reprinted by written permission of copyright holder: Alistair Begg, *truthlines, A Communication to Friends of Truth For Life*, Spring/Summer 1999, (Cleveland, Ohio), p. 1.

[3] Taken from *My Utmost for His Highest* by Oswald Chambers, © 1935 by Dodd Mead & Co., renewed © 1963 by the Chambers Publications Assn., Ltd. Used by permission of Discovery House Publishers, Box 3566, Grand Rapids, MI. All rights reserved. February 9th.

[4] Copyright 1989 Cook Communications Ministries. *The Bible Exposition Commentary Volume 2* by Warren W. Wiersbe. Used with permission, may not be further reproduced. All rights reserved. p. 390.

[5] *Life Application Bible Commentary, 1 &2 Peter and Jude*, (Carol Stream, Illinois: Tyndale House Publishers, Inc., 1995), p. 130.

[6] J. Oswald Sanders, *Spiritual Leadership*, (Moody Bible Institute of Chicago, 1967, 1980), p. 29.

Chapter 5

[1] Don and Katie Fortune, *Discovering Your God-Given Gifts,* (Grand Rapids, Michigan: Chosen Books, 1987), p. 17.

Chapter 6

[1] J. Oswald Sanders, *Spiritual Leadership*, (Moody Bible Institute of Chicago, 1967, 1980), p. 19.

Chapter 7

[1] J. Oswald Sanders, *Spiritual Leadership*, (Moody Bible Institute of Chicago, 1967, 1980), p. 79.

[2] Taken from *My Utmost for His Highest* by Oswald Chambers, © 1935 by Dodd Mead & Co., renewed © 1963 by the Chambers Publications Assn., Ltd. Used by permission of Discovery House Publishers, Box 3566, Grand Rapids, MI. All rights reserved. October 24th.

[3] Frank L. Houghton, *Amy Carmichael of Dohnavur*, (Fort Washington, PA: Christian Literature Crusade, 1953), p. 59

Chapter 8

[1] Funk & Wagnalls Standard Desk Dictionary Volume 1 (Lippincott & Crowell Publishers, 1980), p. 367.
[2] IBID
[3] IBID
[4] Oswald Chambers, *My Utmost For His Highest*, (Uhrichsville, Ohio: Dodd, Mead & Company, Ltd., Discovery House Publishers, 1935), March 27th.
[5] IBID

Chapter 9

[1] Haddon W. Robinson, *Biblical Preaching*, (Grand Rapids: Baker, 1980), p. 41.
[2] Jim Wilhoit and Leland Ryken, *Effective Bible Teaching*, (Grand Rapids Michigan: Baker Book House, 1988), p. 83.
[3] Ibid, p. 114.
[4] Howard G. Hendricks, *Teaching to Change Lives*, (Portland, OR: Multnomah, 1987) p.109.

Chapter 10

[1] Amy Carmichael, *Thou Givest ... They Gather,* (Fort Washington, Pennsylvania: Christian Literature Crusade, 1958), p. 152.

Appendix A

[1] J. Oswald Sanders, *Spiritual Leadership,* (Moody Bible Institute of Chicago, 1967, 1980), p.130.
[2] IBID pp. 127-128

ABOUT THE AUTHOR

Linda has dedicated her life to serving the Lord as a teacher, writer, and speaker. While teaching the Word of God, training leaders, and speaking at retreats and other women's ministry functions, she has also written curriculum for over 20 books of the Bible.

If you would be interested in having more information about her ministry, please visit her blog at www.lindaoborne.wordpress.com, or email her at myutmost1@aol.com.

www.ingramcontent.com/pod-product-compliance
Lightning Source LLC
Chambersburg PA
CBHW060157050426
42446CB00013B/2871